Cultural China

敦煌莫高窟

Dunhuang Mogao Grottos

Zhang Yanmei

Better Link Press

This book is edited and designed by the Editorial Committee of *Cultural China* series

Managing Directors: Wang Youbu, Xu Naiqing
Editorial Director: Wu Ying
Editors: Patrick Wallace, Yang Xinci

Text by Zhang Yanmei
Translation by Han Lei (with Shanghai FESCO International Training Center)

Interior and Cover Design: Yuan Yinchang, Li Jing

ISBN: 978-1-60220-302-0

Address any comments about *Travel through the Middle Kingdom: Dunhuang Mogao Grottos* to:

Better Link Press
99 Park Ave
New York, NY 10016
USA
or
Shanghai Press and Publishing Development Company
F 7 Donghu Road, Shanghai, China (200031)
Email: comments_betterlinkpress@hotmail.com

Computer typeset by Yuan Yinchang Design Studio, Shanghai
Printed in China by Shanghai Donnelley Printing Co. Ltd.

1 2 3 4 5 6 7 8 9 10

CONTENTS

CONTENTS

Foreword

China is known as *Zhong Guo* or Middle Kingdom in Chinese. This term originates from the 10th Century BC when the Zhou Dynasty was defending itself from encroaching barbarians. The Middle Kingdom then stretched from the modern day province of Jiangsu in the east to Sichuan in the west, from Hebei in the north-east and to parts of Gansu in the north-west. The Middle Kingdom was not a nation-state, but the assertion of a unified, highly developed and centralized culture. Cultural relics and artifacts, as well as historical documents from this period, demonstrate how technologically advanced the Middle Kingdom was. From its uniquely sophisticated script to its metallurgical discoveries, the Middle Kingdom had no rivals in the Far East. Silk, magnificent bronzes and jades and Chinese characters all attest to the fact that the Middle Kingdom was the center of civilization. It has maintained its cultural supremacy for thousands of years, its influence spreading to Japan and Korea, and reaching all the way to Vietnam and Indonesia.

The term "Middle Kingdom" has since come to represent one of the oldest civilizations in the world. The Great Wall of China, the Terracotta Warriors of Xi'an and the Forbidden City are just a few of the sites that introduce visitors to the magnificent history and culture of the Middle Kingdom. A walk through Suzhou Gardens, a hike through Yellow Mountain, or a boat ride down the Three Gorges will offer the visitor a more leisurely expedition. Traveling through the Middle Kingdom may sometimes be a challenge, but is always rewarding.

This series aims to offer an in-depth look at some of these famous locations, and to give the discerning traveler detailed descriptions as well as a thorough historical and cultural background. With beautiful illustrations and photographs, you will find our "Travel through the Middle Kingdom" books a most trustworthy companion, and a useful introduction to the wonders of China.

Places of Interest in Dunhuang

Advice for Travelling in Dunhuang

The Best Season for Tourism in Dunhuang

Dunhuang is a desert city, isolated by both mountain ranges and great distances from any source of humid ocean air. As such, it is extremely arid and seldom has any precipitation. There can also be sharp differences in temperature during the day and night, so often a heavy coat might be necessary at night, while a thin shirt might be enough for the daytime. Since most visitors find Dunhuang intolerably cold in winter, the tourist season runs from March to November. The best time for traveling there is from May to September.

Tips

Transport:

- A taxi from downtown Dunhuang to the Mogao Grottos will cost about 35 RMB. Rental cars and buses with drivers are also available, but the cost is a bit higher.
- For returning to Dunhuang, it is often possible to have the taxi or rental car wait to take you back, but this should be negotiated in advance and can be expensive. A cheaper alternative would be the public transport for people who work at or near the Mogao Grottos. Minibus service returning to Dunhuang begins at 6 pm. It costs 5 RMB per person.

Admission Fee:

- 100 RMB to visit a selection of caves, the Cultural Relics Protection and Exhibition Center, and the Manuscript Exhibition Hall.
- In order to visit special caves or caves currently not on the itinerary, visitors may have to pay extra fees.

Hours:

Spring, summer and autumn: 8 am–6 pm daily
Winter: 9 am–4:30 pm daily

Sharing from Experience:

- Since Dunhuang is very hot in summer and can experience heavy wind and sandstorms, sunglasses, a good sunblock, lip balm, a hat, handkerchiefs and other protective gear are advisable.
- The Mogao Grottos are not open on overcast or rainy days, so when arranging your trip you should take the weather into consideration.
- The Mogao Grottos face east, and each cave has a protective door and no interior

lighting. Most caves will therefore require a flashlight if you wish to see anything. These can be brought from outside or rented at the Grottos.

- The total number of visitors allowed per day is limited and the natural lighting conditions are relatively better before noon, so it is best to come early in the day.
- English-speaking guides are sometimes available, but on a first-come-first-serve basis. To enhance your chance of getting an English-speaking guide, it is often better to arrive at opening time.
- Apart from the Mogao Grottos, other activities in or around Dunhuang include climbing the Mingsha Dunes, camel riding, and paragliding.

Local Delicacies

The Three Treasures of Anxi

The three local delicacies considered unique to the region around Dunhuang are suoyang wine, honeydew melons, and Shuangta fish. Suoyang wine is made from *suoyang*, a rare medicinal herb that gave the city of Suoyang its name. Honeydew melons of Guazhou District boast a history of over 3000 years, and are the food of legend. Freshwater fish from the Shuangta Reservoir are famous for their smooth and refreshing taste.

Hand-Made *Saozi* Noodles

Saozi noodles are made by rolling out pastry as thin as a piece of paper. This is then sliced into thin noodles. The noodles are served in different kinds of spicy or sour soups accompanied by different meats or vegetables, or other special ingredients depending upon the locality. *Saozi* noodles are always served during festivals and the New Year's, or when welcoming honored guests, as they represent a special delicacy to the people of Dunhuang.

Dunhuang *Niangpizi*

Dunhuang *niangpizi* has a long history as a folk snack. To make it, water and flour are first mixed together evenly. This paste is then thinned with water. After being thinned, the paste is spread uniformly onto an iron plate and briefly cooked like a thin crepe or pancake. It is then braising in boiling water for about one minute. Finally, it is sliced and served with a little mustard, garlic juice, green pepper, soy sauce, and vinegar.

Introduction

In the far west of China is Gansu Province. There, 25 kilometers Southeast from the city of Dunhuang, set against a cliff abutting the Mingsha Dunes, there is long zigzag network of plank paths leading to more than 500 caves. These are the Mogao Grottos, one of the largest sites of Buddhist art in the world. Work on the the Mogao Grottos, known locally as "Thousand Buddha Caves", began in 366 A.D., giving the caves a history of more than 1,600 years.

In the second century B.C., Zhang Qian, a general of the Western Han Dynasty, was dispatched to the Western Regions. This opened up a trade route from east to west known as the Silk Road. As an important crossroad of trade, both merchants and envoys used Dunhuang as a stopover point on the Silk Road, giving Dunhuang a strategic place in history.

During the Eastern Han Dynasty, Buddhism was introduced through the Silk Road to China. Located at the west end of the Silk Road, the seeds of Buddhism were planted in Dunhuang earlier than other areas of China. It began to flower in the Eastern Jin Dynasty, when a number of eminent monks practiced Buddhism, delivered sermons, and translated Buddhist sutras in Dunhuang. It came to full blossom in Dunhuang during the Wei, Jin, Southern and Northern Dynasties, when Dunhuang turned into one of the main cultural centers for Buddhism.

With the ever-growing popularity of Buddhism in the Hexi Corridor, many temples and caves were built. These include the Mount Maiji Grottos of Tianshui Prefecture, the Binling Grottos of Yongjing Prefecture (West Qin Dynasty), the Wuwei Grottos at Mount Tianti (North Liang Dynasty), the Grottos in Jinta Temple in Zhangye Prefecture (Northern Liang Dynasty), and the Grottos of Mount Wenshu of Jiuquan Prefecture (Northern Liang Dynasty). Since it was a popular custom in the region to create grottos for Buddhist worship, it is of no wonder that grottos were also dug by the banks of Dangquan River in Dunhuang. These caves, the Mogao Grottos, were popular through a thousand years of history and a dozen dynasties.

By the time of the Yuan Dynasty, the Dunhuang Mogao Grottos had become a meeting place of Buddhist culture and art, with an endless stream of pilgrims coming to it. However, during the Ming Dynasty, Dunhuang was abandoned and history passed it by. Even though the rulers of the early Qing Dynasty regained control over Dunhuang and regions west of it, the prosperity the Silk Road enjoyed during the Han and Tang Dynasties could never be recovered. No more caves have been carved since the Ming Dynasty. The brilliance of Dunhuang in former days became lost in history.

In the middle of the 19th century, the Mogao Grottos were in a state of decay and ruin. Most of the plank paths in front of the caves were damaged. The lowest tier of caves was buried in sand dunes because it had not been cleaned or maintained. Standing against the front of the caves were three crumbling temples. The two higher temples were the residences of a handful of Buddhist lamas, while the lowest temple, located on the bottom tier of caves, was inhabited by Wang Yuanlu, a Daoist priest who wanted to change it into a Daoist temple.

One day in 1900, someone was cleaning the sand from out of the adjoining cave to this lower temple, the cave now known as Cave 16, when a gap split open in the northern wall of the corridor in the cave. This gap caught little attention. Later, an old worker hired by Wang Yuanlu was copying scriptures in the corridor. When he felt tired, he would use a bunch of long hay to light his pipe. Once, after lighting his tobacco, he conveniently inserted the burnt hay into the gap in the wall. To his surprise, he discovered that the gap appeared almost bottomless. Curiously, some sort of echo like a drumbeat could be heard when he knocked on the wall with his pipe. He brought this to the attention of Wang Yuanlu. That night, Wang Yuanlu dug through the sealing clay along the gap, and found a small cave that had been hidden. In the shimmering light, he could see thousands upon thousands of manuscripts piled up. These ancient manuscripts are now called the Dunhuang manuscripts in academic circles, and were unearthed from what is known today as Cave 17, or the Cache of Manuscripts.

The middle part of the Dunhuang Mogao Grottos

When the contents of Cave 17 are taken together

The Lower Temple

The decorative archway (Qing Dynasty) which serves as the Main Entrance for visitors

with all of the other artifacts at Dunhuang, the result is a cultural treasure house containing more than 45,000 square meters of murals, over 2,000 painted statues, more than 50,000 manuscripts, and nearly 1,000 woodcuts, along with various other silk paintings, embroideries and other works of art. There is no place other than Dunhuang where the art work of so many different dynasties through more than 1,000 years of history has been so well-preserved. There is also no place other than Dunhuang where such a huge amount of art treasures have been kept so completely intact.

When visiting Dunhuang, you will marvel at the magnificent murals, splendid and beautiful statues, fine architecture, and unrivalled cultural relics. The ancient artists and craftsmen at Dunhuang combined the architecture, sculpture, and painting techniques and styles from central China with those of western regions, creating Buddhist art work with Chinese characteristics. As a result of this synthesis of foreign and national art forms, the Buddhist art at the Dunhuang Mogao Grottos not only provides us with valuable reference material for the study of ancient Chinese politics, economy, culture, religion, and international relations, but also leaves us with a precious treasure for understanding the history and development of Buddhism. For these reasons, in December 1987, the Dunhuang Mogao Grottos were added to UNESCO's World Heritage List.

The Early Period

Northern Dynasties

One day during the second year of the Jianyuan Era of the Former Qin Dynasty, a monk named Le Zun was traveling from the east to Dunhuang when he stopped to take a rest. Sitting in meditation, he suddenly saw thousands of shafts of light streaming down from the nearby Mount Sanwei. To him, these shafts of light looked like thousands of incarnations of Buddha. At that moment, Le Zun decided to dig a cave near that spot for worship and meditation.

Panorama of the Mogao Grottos and the location of the Northern Dynasties caves

A moonlit night over the Mingsha Dunes

Some ten kilometers east from the city of Dunhuang, you will find the serpentine Mount Sanwei standing amidst the gravel of the Gobi Desert. Go another ten kilometers south, and you will see the Gobi to the left and soft sand leading to the Mingsha Dunes to the right. The Dangquan River, really just a small stream, flows between the two, forming a small oasis along its banks. Cross the stone bridge over the Dangquan River, and you will go through a memorial arch. The Chinese characters inscribed on it say, Shishi Baozang, meaning "Stone Chambers and Treasures". Walk another 30 meters and you will see a second memorial arch standing before you. This is the main entrance of the Mogao Grottos.

The Mogao Grottos are carved into the side of a cliff that runs from north to south. Stretching for more than 1,600 meters, the four tiers of caves are connected to each other by plank paths. The main section of

The Mingsha Dunes and Yueya Spring

the Mogao Grottos, in the south, numbers 492 extant caves. Most of these have murals or statues inside. Since 1991, a thorough excavation and survey of the caves in the northern area has been carried out by the Dunhuang Research Institute of Cultural Relics, resulting in the identification of yet another 200 caves. Most of these caves, however, are devoid of any artifacts or art work.

Nirvana

In Buddhism, nirvana means a transcendent state in which there is no suffering, desire, or sense of self. It is the state of perfect blessedness achieved by extinction of individual existence and by the absorption of the soul into the supreme spirit, or by the extinction of all desires and passions. It is the final goal of Buddhism.

Sunrise over Mount Sanwei

The Earliest Grottos —Meditation Caves

Inscriptions in the Mogao Grottos dating from the Tang Dynasty state that construction began in 366 A.D., when a monk from central China named Le Zun was traveling through Dunhuang. While deep in meditation, he suddenly witnessed thousands of shafts of light streaming down from Mount Sanwei. To him, these shafts of light looked like a myriad of Buddhas. He then became determined to carve a cave there to meditate in. Shortly afterwards, Fa Liang, another monk, dug a second cave in the area. Soon, a growing number of people came here to dig caves there, and the Mogao Grottos became a known center for Buddhist meditation.

The section of the Mogao Grottos in the north

Early caves built for the purpose of meditation, an important practice in Buddhism, are quite prevalent at the Mogao Grottos. Preserved on the second tier in the middle of the Grottos is a small series of interconnected meditation caves (or *chanku* caves). The main hall (Cave 268) is narrow with a niche in the back wall containing a statue of Buddha. Both the side walls of the main hall have two small chambers carved into them (Caves 267, 269-271). Each chamber contains a mere one cubic meter of space–only enough room for one person sitting or kneeling down inside. Meditation rooms used by ancient monks, these are the oldest extant caves among the Mogao Grottos.

Caves of the Northern Liang Dynasty

During the Northern Liang Dynasty (397-439 A.D.), the development of Buddhism in China reached a peak. The rulers of the Northern Liang Dynasty not only advocated preaching Buddhism, but also expended huge

Background Notes on the Bodhisattva in Meditation

The Bodhisattva in Meditation represents the image of Sakyamuni in his quest to overcome the sufferings of birth, old age, sickness and death before he achieved enlightenment. This image is usually of a sitting figure with his upper torso slightly leaning forward, his right elbow on his lap and his fingers propping up his jaw, looking downwards as if deep in thought.

King Sibi feeding a hawk with his own flesh to save a pigeon, Cave 275, northern wall

amounts of money to build temples and dig religious grottos. Under these circumstances, Caves 268, 272, and 275 were constructed.

The representative cave of this period, Cave 275, contains a 3.4 meter-high statue of Maitreya the Bodhisattva against the back wall. This is one of the largest statues in the world surviving from this time period. The Bodhisattva sits between two lions, upright on a chair with a triangle-shaped backrest. A bejeweled coronet crowns his head, a garland circles his neck, and a *dhoti* girds his loins. His feet are crossed and he has a round, graceful face with a tranquil expression. His robust physique, large nose, and round eyes display characteristics not usually found in the people of central China. The carving techniques themselves show the influence of Ghandaran art. On either side of the cave are two small niches located near the top of the walls. The ones nearest the Bodhisattva

Background Notes on Tusita Heaven

Tusita Heaven is the fourth of six different heavens in Buddhist cosmology. This is Maitreya's home until the time of his future arrival on the Earth. In Tusita Heaven, 500 trillion sons of heaven reside in 500 trillion treasure palaces from which 500 trillion shafts of light radiate, with lotus flowers and treasure trees inside. The inhabitants there are entertained by 500 trillion flying *apsaras* playing wonderful music. In later Buddhist cosmology, Tusita Heaven became associated with the Pure Land, which is central to the thinking of Pure Land Buddhism.

Interior of Cave 275

are shaped as watchtowers and contain statues of Maitreya reminiscent of the main statue. The two furthest are vaulted niches containing statues of Bodhisattvas in Meditation.

Nearly the entire surface of the walls and ceiling of the cave was painted in colorful murals, much of which still survives. The murals depicting various *jataka* on the northern wall of the cave are particularly striking. *Jakata* are ancient Buddhist fables and parables, mostly about the events in the life of Buddha during his many reincarnations. These *jataka* are tales of Sakyamuni (i.e., Buddha) in his previous incarnations as he endured humiliation, and sacrificed himself in order to achieve unsurpassed enlightenment. They include *the jakata of King Bilengkali willingly being nailed at a thousand places on his body*, *King Sibi feeding a hawk a piece of his own flesh in order to save a pigeon*, and *King Chandraprabha donating his head to a heretic*. While the illustrations of *jataka* in the Mogao Grottos seem gory by modern standards, mostly regarding sacrifice or death, they were intended to highlight a spirit of benevolence and compassion, and to illustrate the Buddhist conception of boundless nobility and holiness.

From a technical standpoint, the artistic techniques used in these murals betray the influence of Ghandaran art. The use of single-frame paintings to describe full stories is rarely found in later murals at Mogao.

Background Notes on Ghandara

Ghandara refers to what is now eastern Afghanistan and Peshawar in Pakistan. Part of the Yuezhi Tribe, a people group originally from the Hexi Corridor area of northwest China's Gansu Province, migrated west and became known as the Kushans. They established rule over Ghandara in the first century. The greatest king of the Kushans was Kanishka (2nd century). He was a great patron of Buddhism, constructed many temples, pagodas and Buddhist statues within his territory, and bringing about a regional shift towards Buddhism as the main religion. Previously, Ghandara had been ruled by the Greeks, who brought with them many aspects of their culture. This resulted in Ghandara in an intermingling of Hellenistic and Indian artistic styles that can clearly be seen in Buddhist statuary of this era, and heavily influencing Buddhist artwork throughout the region.

Interior of Cave 254

Caves with Central Columns (Northern Wei Dynasty)

The Northern Wei Dynasty spanned 148 years (386-534 A.D.). During the later period of the Northern Wei Dynasty, Yuan Rong, a follower of Buddhism, took up post as the prefectural governor of Dunhuang. He wished to strengthen his own governing authority by engaging in

Buddhist ceremonies and services on a large scale. Consequently, massive construction of the Mogao Grottos was conducted.

During this time, most of the caves built had a central column originating in style from caitya caves, also known as a stupa temple caves. In ancient India, stupas were often enshrined in the center of caves, which were accordingly called "stupa halls". As time passed, statues of Buddha replaced stupas as objects of worship, resulting in changes to the form of the stupa halls. By the time of the fourth and fifth centuries, when this cave style was introduced to the western regions, it no longer had a stupa inside but had a central column in front of which a statue would be placed. This style prevailed during the Northern Wei, Western Wei and Northern Zhou Dynasties. The most representative caves of the Northern Wei Dynasty at the Mogao Grottos are Caves 254, 257, and 259.

Cave 254

Outside the door of Cave 254, the railings of ancient plank paths are still preserved. In the center of the cave is a square column with niches in all four directions. Each niche enshrines a statue of Buddha, allowing devotees of Buddhism to circle the central column and pay homage from each side.

Niches in the form of ancient watchtowers were carved on the upper portion of the central column in southern, western and northern

Background Notes on the Niches

The niches where statues of Buddha or Bodhisattvas are enshrined can be divided into several categories according to shapes: watchtower shape, round vaulted shape, double-tier shape, open-mouth shape, and so forth.

directions as well as the two flanking walls. Watchtower niches were meant to resemble the watchtowers commonly constructed near the gates of fortifications, palaces and castles after the Qin and Han Dynasties. These were not only common structures during that time, but were also symbols of power. In Buddhism, the watchtower niches are meant to evoke the idea that the caves are in a world of heavenly palaces.

The front of the cave has a ceiling in the shape of an inverted "V", a style characteristic of the earlier Han Dynasty. A crossbeam with rafters trailing down from it is painted on the ceiling. At each end of the ceiling beams, support blocks have been carved in the rock. These resemble wooden *dougong*, a typical feature of Chinese traditional architecture. The crossbeam, rafters and *dougong* serve no practical value. However, they reminded people of the familiar features of their own homes, thus narrowing the gap between common people and Buddhism. The remainder of the ceiling is carved and painted as a caisson, another constituent component of Chinese traditional architecture. Intricate patterns of lotus and honeysuckle are painted in the caisson, as if to give life to the cold cave.

The *jakata* paintings on the southern and northern walls bear the strong influence of Ghandara. The painting of *Prince Mahasattva feeding himself to the tigers* is meant to be illustrative of a spirit of sacrifice. In the fable, the King of Baodian, a country in ancient India, had three sons, the youngest of whom was named Mahasattva. One day they went to a forest. On the road back to the palace, the three princes saw a tigress and her cubs, which were starving to death. Resolving to save these tigers, Prince Mahasattva quietly left his two brothers. He returned to the tigress and her cubs and stretched himself out for them to eat. However, the tigers were too weak from hunger even to bite the prince.

Mural illustrating the *jataka* of Prince Mahasattva, Cave 254, southern wall

Mahasattva was so concerned he climbed onto a cliff overhanging the tigers, used a stick to pierce his neck, and then jumped off. He fell in front of the tigress and her cubs. After gradually resuming strength by licking up the prince's dripping blood, they ate up the rest of his flesh.

When the other two princes realized that their little brother Mahasattva was missing, they rushed back to the mountain, only to find the remains of Mahasattva's body. They then knew that Prince Mahasattva had sacrificed himself to save the tigers. In deep sorrow, they came back to the palace and told what had happened to the King. The King and the Queen grieved for their son greatly. The two brothers collected the remains of Prince Mahasattva, and built a stupa to his memory. It was said that Mahasattva was a previous incarnation of Sakyamuni, and that because Sakyamuni sacrificed himself so many times in previous lives it was possible for him to attain enlightenment.

The painting presents the whole tragedy as a tableau. The three brothers stand in the center of this tableau, looking downwards at the tigress biting at the dead body. On the right of the tableau, we can see Mahasattva piercing his neck and then jumping off the cliff. The tableau's compact composition and strong hues bring about a dramatic visual effect, making this one of the outstanding examples of *jakata* paintings from early times.

Another painting in the cave is based upon *The jakata of King Sibi* feeding a hawk a piece of his own flesh in order to save a pigeon. King Sibi was famous in ancient times for his philanthropic and benevolent work. One day, a hawk was chasing a pigeon. The pigeon, in great danger, asked for King Sibi's help.

King Sibi said to the hawk, "I am determined to save all living things. I do not want you to take this pigeon."

The hawk responded, "I will die of hunger if I let the pigeon go. Why is the pigeon more important for you to save than I?"

"I will offer you some other food instead," the king answered.

"Fresh blood and meat are the only food that I can eat," the hawk replied.

At that moment, King Sibi resolved to offer his own flesh to the hawk in order to save the pigeon. He cut off a piece of his flesh. However, when this flesh was weighed, it was lighter than that of the pigeon. Consequently, the king himself sat on the scale, deciding to feed his whole body to the hawk. Immediately, the universe began shaking and all of the flesh that had been cut off suddenly returned to the King's body. Sakra, the god who controls the thunder, lightning, wind, and rain, and his ministers suddenly revealed themselves.

"Congratulations!" Sakra said. "You have attained unsurpassed enlightenment. We took the form of the hawk and the pigeon in order to test you. Sure enough, you demonstrated a firm willingness to endure humiliation and show unbounded benevolence. You will become a Buddha in future."

To show how King Sibi manifested a spirit of kindness, magnanimity and resoluteness, the cave painting displays King Sibi with his head leaning slightly forward. The pigeon is in one hand, while the other hand is raised to stop the hawk.

Cave 257

Most of the pitched ceiling of Cave 257 has collapsed or has been damaged. However, a long mural scrolls around the central portion of the southern, western and northern walls. Several *jakata* are illustrated on this mural, including that of *A novice Stamanera committing suicide to protect his virtue, The story of the nine-colored deer, The story of Sumati burning incense to invoke Buddha's blessing.*

The most notable of these is that of the nine-colored deer. This *jataka* is a story of a beautiful deer living by the bank of the Ganges River. As the name implies, this deer was special because its fur had a pattern of nine different colors. One day, the deer was wandering along the banks of the Ganges when it suddenly heard someone screaming. The deer looked and saw a man struggling in the water, so it risked its own life to jump in and rescue the man from drowning.

Grateful to the deer for saving his life, the man wanted to somehow repay him.

The deer said calmly, "I need nothing in return. I only want you to keep my whereabouts a secret."

As the man was returning home, he saw many people surrounding a

The king leaving the city in search of the nine-colored deer, Cave 257, western wall

notice on the city gate. It turned out that the Queen had had a dream in which she saw a gorgeous deer of nine colors. When she woke up, the Queen told the King about her dream and asked him to capture the deer so that she could make a dress out of its skin. Thereupon, the King issued an edict offering half of his land and countless wealth to anyone who could help capture the deer. On hearing about the reward, the man who had been saved by the deer became greedy. Breaking his oath, he went and told the king where the deer was.

The next day, the man led the King and his army to the forest where the deer lived near the banks of the Ganges. At that time, the nine-colored deer was asleep. One of the deer's good friends, a crow, tried to wake it up, but it was too late as the nine-colored deer found itself surrounded on all sides by the king's troops. On seeing the man whose

Mural illustrating the *jataka* of the nine-colored deer, Cave 257, western wall

life it had saved, the deer realized what had happened. The deer told the King the whole story of rescuing the man. Touched, the King said, "Even the deer, an animal, is conscious of good and evil. How can we human beings do such treacherous things?" Thereupon, the King ordered the deer released, and banned anyone from harming it.

In this painting, the composition has shifted from that of single-frame with only a few story elements, to that of a sequence of scenes that display the entire development of the story. These scenes scroll from the ends of the mural to the center where the final scene is presented, focusing on a depiction of the deer which is meant to emphasize its integrity and kindness. This innovation in how the paintings were composed is of great importance to the development of *jakata* paintings. This style of composition soon became predominate, culminating during the Northern Zhou Dynasty, when many outstanding works emerged.

Cave 259

The front ceiling of Cave 259 has collapsed and has been severely damaged. Only half of this relatively small cave now remains. Nevertheless, the delicate statues in this cave are well-preserved. Outstanding among these are statues of Sakyamuni and Prabhutaratna displayed in the front niche, sitting side-by-side preaching. Another niche contains one of the more famous statues of the Mogao Grottos, a lifelike statue of a meditating Buddha in a cassock. The contemplative expression in his eyes and the composed and tranquil mood suggest his full consciousness of enlightenment. His gentle smile has often been remarked upon and likened to that of the Mona Lisa.

Painted statue of a meditating Buddha, Cave 259, northern wall

Images of Fuxi and Nüwa (in Chinese mythology, the god and goddess that propagated the human race), Cave 285, eastern slope of the ceiling

The Waning of Foreign Influences (Western Wei Dynasty)

The Western Wei Dynasty was established in 535 A.D. While many foreign factors influenced the art of the Northern Wei Dynasty, during the Western Wei Dynasty the caves began the large-scale incorporation of artistic elements more typically representative of central China. This gives the caves of the Western Wei Dynasty a distinctive style best represented by Caves 249 and 285.

Interior of Cave 249

Interior of Cave 288

Mural of a celestial musician playing a *konghou* (a kind of harp), Cave 285, southern wall

Mural of a hunting scene, Cave 249, northern slope of the ceiling

Cave 249

Cave 249 is a rectangular room with a ceiling in the shape of an inverted "U", also known as an inverted-dipper ceiling. The upper portions the walls are covered with paintings of celestial musicians, and the lower portions with paintings of thousands of Buddhas and donor Bodhisattvas.

Background Notes on Flying *Apsaras*

In Buddhism, *apsaras* are celestial figures much like angels that can fly freely in the sky. The origin of *apsaras* is unclear. They are often presented in artwork showering flower petals or playing musical instruments. Since this accords with the roles of Ghandharvas and Kinnara (two different kinds of spirits known for their musical abilities), some believe that the *apsaras* are merely manifestations of these beings.

Flying *apsaras*, Cave 249, northern wall

The content and layout of these murals are all evocative of the Northern Wei Dynasty. However, new elements include paintings of Xiwangmu ("The Queen of the West", an important deity in Daoism) with her attendants on the southern slope of the ceiling, and Dongwanggong ("The Prince of the East", Xiwangmu's royal consort) on the northern slope. These paintings from Chinese mythology share similarities to reliefs and murals of Xiwangmu and Dongwanggong found in tombs from the Han Dynasty. Dongwanggong is seated in a chariot drawn by dragons and guided by celestial beings. He is accompanied by a celestial figure with feathered arms and flying *apsaras*. His wife Xiwangmu is seated in a chariot drawn by phoenixes and escorted by winged fish. She is followed

Background Notes on Donors

Donors were literally just that–people who regularly donated alms to Buddhist monks or nuns. Through the giving of alms, a donor is thought to accrue some of the same spiritual blessing that the person they are giving to already has obtained. On the other hand, without donors, Buddhist temples, monasteries, and religious complexes like the Mogao Grottos could not thrive. To celebrate this relationship and to honor the donors who supported them, the artist-monks who created the Mogao Grottos often incorporated images of their donors into their art work.

by celestial beings, including a *kaiming*, which has the head of a human and the body of a dragon.

On the eastern slope of the ceiling, two demigods hold the *mani* jewel. A *mani* jewel is also known as the wish-granting jewel. In Buddhism, the *mani* jewel has the power to bring salvation. Beneath these figures are Zhuque, the mythical red bird that serves as the guardian of the south, and Xuanwu, a creature which is half tortoise and half snake and serves as the guardian of the north. Figures of the Three Emperors from Chinese legend–Sui Ren, Fu Xi, and Shen Nong are respectively depicted on the eastern, southern and northern slopes of the ceiling. The inclusion of King Asura, a Hindu diety, on the western slope flanked by the gods of thunder, lightning, the wind, and the rain, perfectly demonstrating the nature of Buddhist syncretism at Mogao.

The southern and northern walls have preaching scenes with the Buddha standing on the central lotus pond surrounded on both sides by Bodhisattvas and flying *apsaras*. The *apsaras* flying above wear loose gowns with long sleeves, typical of the clothing worn in central China during the time. However, the *apsaras* covering the lower portions of the wall display a more typically foreign influence. Most interestingly, a *taotie* flanked by two dragons was portrayed at the center of the painted canopy over the Preaching Buddha on the southern wall, while another *taotie* flanked by phoenixes can be found in the same position over the Preaching Buddha on the north wall. The *taotie* is mythological creature whose face or head is commonly found as a decorative motif on items from ancient China. Mythical creatures such as the *taotie*, dragon, and phoenix are all typical Chinese motifs, just like the figures on the ceilings of the cave. This demonstrates once again how traditional figures from Chinese mythology were incorporated with those of Buddhism.

Cave 285

Cave 285 is a standard meditation cave. The rectangular main hall features an inverted-dipper ceiling. The back wall has a large niche in the center with a statue of Buddha inside, flanked by two small niches with statues of meditating monks. The main hall has four small meditation rooms on either side, each of which can only shelter one person.

The northern wall of this cave has eight murals containing preaching scenes. Below each painting, an invocation is inscribed, along with depictions of donors. The invocations in the cave state that this cave was constructed during the fourth and fifth years of the Datong Era (538-539 A.D.). This is the earliest written record regarding the chronology of the caves.

Painted statue of a meditating monk, Cave 285, southern niche of the western wall

The images of the Buddha in this cave are quite different from that those of the Northern Wei Dynasty. Portraits of Buddha from earlier times often featured a robust figure with a naked upper torso draped with tassels or ribbons. These Buddhas are slim, have thin faces and open eyes, and all wear loose gowns with long sleeves. Above their portraits, lithe *apsaras* float through the air, bringing vitality to the paintings.

Most of the donors depicted below the preaching scenes look the same, making these symbolic representations of Buddhist

Mural of a preaching scene, Cave 285, eastern wall

Portraits of Buddhist donors, Cave 285, northern wall

worshippers rather than portraits of real people. However, there are exceptions. For example, among these donors a noblewoman is depicted. In one hand she holds an incense burner, in the other a lotus flower. Facing the Buddha, she has a wispy bun of hair, delicate eyebrows, and rouged cheeks. The drape of her gown and its loose sleeves suggest that she is about to lift off the ground and begin flying in the sky with ease. This image is much like that of Luoshen, a goddess, in the painting *The Ode to Luoshen* by Gu Kaizhi (344-406 A.D.). This demonstrates the impact of the Southern Dynasties on the mural art of the Mogao Grottos.

On the southern wall of Cave 285, a painting tells the story of five hundred bandits being converted to Buddhism. In this tale, a gang of bandits often robbed travelers. When captured by soldiers, the bandits were sentenced to death by torture. After having their noses cut off and

Left: Mural illustrating the conversion to Buddhism of the five hundred bandits, Cave 285, southern wall

their eyes gouged out, the suffering bandits cried out in remorse for their actions and in sorrow for their fate. At that moment, Buddha came and preached to them. The five hundred bandits consequently converted to Buddhism and became monks. Buddha brought them medicine that healed their wounds and restored their sight. The story is presented on a rolling sequence of scenes which portray in detail not just figures, but also buildings, distant mountains, trees, ponds, birds, and beasts.

The Emergence of Palace Caves (Northern Zhou Dynasty)

The Northern Zhou Dynasty was established in 577 A.D. During this period, artistic elements common to central China were further intermingled with foreign elements, but the themes and style of the artwork developed in a different manner compared to the previous eras. Buddhism during this time period gradually attached more importance to the study of sermons and sutras, and less importance to meditation and the practice of *dharma* (the path to enlightenment). Consequently, meditation caves were no longer built, and the number of the caves with central columns declined. The predominant style became that of halls reminiscent of those found in ancient Chinese palaces. For main chambers, these caves have

Mural illustrating the *jataka* of Sudhana, Cave 428

square rooms with a niche at the back in which a statue of Buddha is enshrined. He is flanked by his disciples, Bodhisattvas, Heavenly Kings, and demigods, all arranged in hierarchical order around the Buddha, in exactly the same way the emperors, ministers and servants would stand while he was holding court from his throne. This style reflects the common understanding of Buddhism during the Northern Zhou Dynasty.

Jakatas played an important role in the murals of the Mogao Grottos from the Northern Zhou Dynasty. A noticeable trend among these *jakata* murals is the increasing theme of filial piety. The *jakata* murals include stories such as the one about *Prince Kalyanakari going to sea in search of the mani jewel*, and *The story of Sujata* in Cave 296, and *The story of Sudhana* in Cave 428. These *jakata* all reflect the ideas of filial piety and

Interior of Cave 428

benevolence, ideas which conformed to the government's advocacy of Confucianism.

After Buddhism was introduced to China, it was propagated by intentionally choosing stories and elements that were relatively easy to be understood by the Chinese people in the light of their culture, history, and traditional way of thinking. This is one important reason why Buddhism, as a foreign religion, could develop and grow in China.

Cave 296

The *jakata* of Prince Kalyanakari going to the sea in search of the *mani* jewel, illustrated in Cave 296, goes as follows. The King

Mural illustrating Buddha's life, Cave 290, ceiling

of Varannasi, an ancient Indian state, had two sons, Kalyanakari and Aghakari. Kalyanakari was a kindhearted youth who often opened up his treasure chests and warehouses to give charity to the poor. By and by, the royal coffers became empty. Kalyanakari decided to go to sea to seek the *mani* jewel. When Aghakari learned of this, he joined the expedition, and the two princes set out to sea in two giant ships. On their journey, they discovered a mountain of gold and a mountain of silver. Out of greed, Aghakari overloaded his ship and it capsized. However, Kalyanakari resolutely pressed on, finally arriving at Nagarajas's Palace, the palace of the guardian deity of the ocean, where he acquired the *mani* jewel.

On his way back to Varannasi, Kalyanakari met his brother Aghakari. Discovering that Kalyanakari had acquired the *mani* jewel, Aghakari used poison to blind him. He stole the *mani* jewel and returned to the

Interior of Cave 290

Varannasi alone, lying to the others that Prince Kalyanakari had died. He buried the *mani* jewel in a secret location and told no one that he had it.

Kalyanakari was sleeping at the time of the incident and did not know what had happen or who had blinded him. Gradually dying because of the poison, his life was saved when a shepherd came along and had a bull lick the poison out of his eyes. The shepherd brought the blind prince to the country of Lishiba, and gave him a *konghou* for use to make a living. Every day, Kalyanakari wandered the streets playing the *konghou* and begging for food. The King's gardener hired him to scare away the birds in his orchard. In his leisure at his new job, Kalyanakari played the *konghou* to amuse himself.

One day, a princess taking a walk in the orchard heard Kalyanakari playing the *konghou*. Afterwards, she began coming to the orchard to listen to him play. Soon, she fell in love with the blind young man and wanted to marry him. The King did not agree at first. However, the princess was so determined that the King finally gave in. The princess and Kalyanakari got married. Because of this marriage, his story became known to all, even spreading as far as Varannasi. Discovering that Kalyanakari was still live, his father had him brought home and sent the whole kingdom to greet his arrival.

From the very beginning, the King of Varannasi had been very doubtful of Aghakari's story. On hearing that Kalyanakari was still alive, he had put Aghakari into jail. However, Kalyanakari begged the King to set Aghakari free. On seeing how Kalyanakari had returned good for evil, Aghakari felt ashamed. He handed over the *mani* jewel which he had buried to Kalyanakari, who built a shrine for it. From then on, whenever the people had a need, they prayed to the *mani* jewel, and Varannasi became increasingly prosperous.

The Golden Era

Sui and Tang Dynasties

During the Sui and Tang Dynasties, the rectangular ceilings of the caves were usually in the shape of an inverted "U". Each cave generally had a front and back hall. The front halls had wooden walls installed outside them. On the eaves of these walls, placards described what was in the caves with phrases such as, "From top to bottom, like hanging clouds", or, "With flying pavilions from south to north, connected by colored clouds". The scene at the Mogao Grottos must have seemed like a celestial abode to travelers who had just emerged from the boundless Gobi Desert.

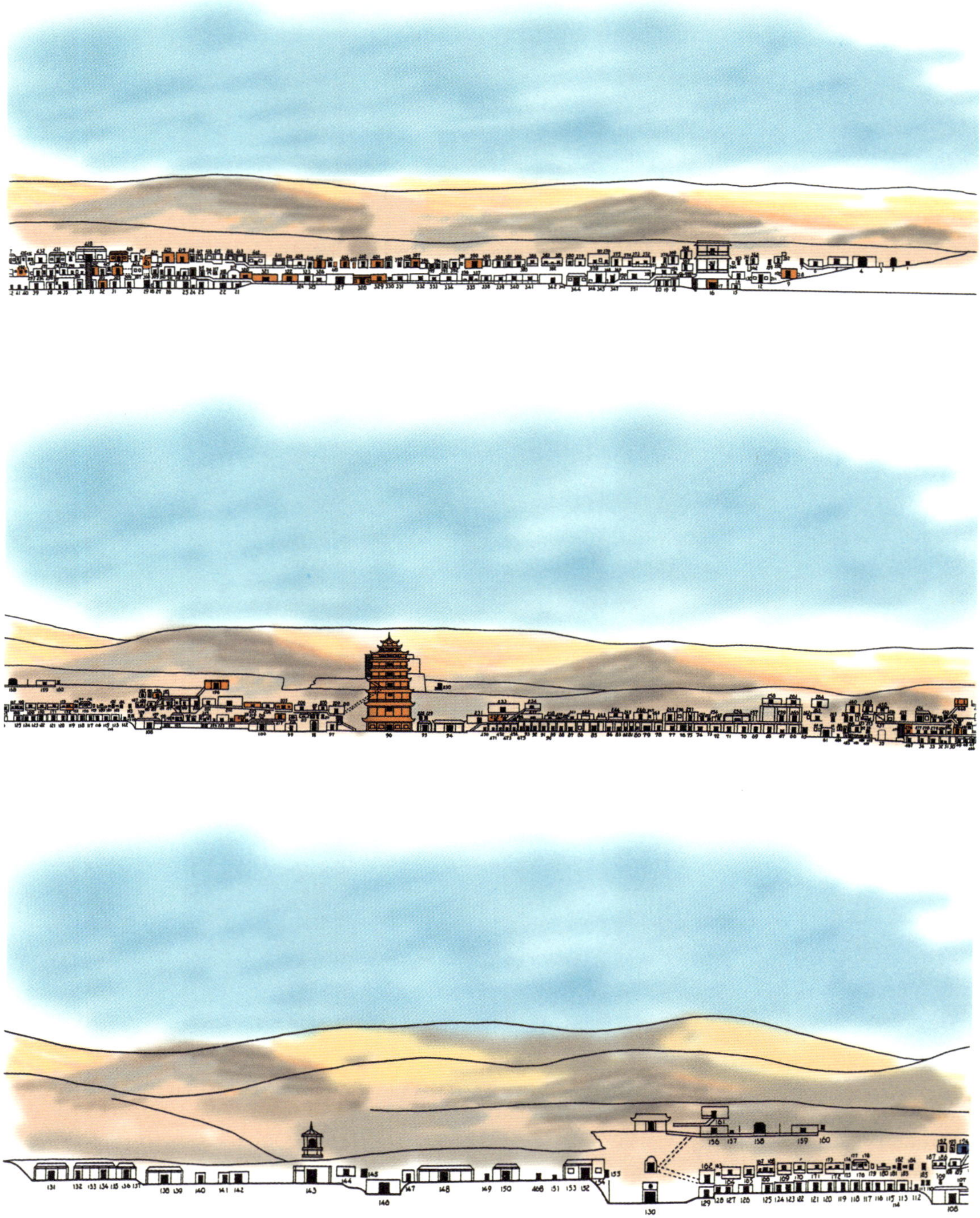

Panorama of the Mogao Grottos and the location of the Sui and Tang Dynasties caves

The Sui and Tang Dynasties (581-907 A.D.) were the golden age of Chinese feudalism, marking the high tide of its economic, political and cultural development. During this period, the Silk Road flourished like never before. Positioned on a conjunction of the Silk Road, Dunhuang served as an important outpost for international trade. Countless numbers of envoys, merchants, monks and priests came and went. Merchants passing through prayed for their safe trip at the Mogao Grottos, donating money and valuables as a sign of righteousness and to accumulate merit. These donations became the material and economic foundation for the subsequent construction of the caves at Mogao. High-ranking officials and the wealthy from the local towns also contributed to the construction of new caves in order to show off their wealth and to honor their ancestors. Indeed, after the Tang Dynasty, a good many caves were transformed into clan halls for individual families.

Many new caves were constructed during the Sui and Tang Dynasties, of which more than 90 are still extant from the Sui Dynasty, and 232 from the Tang Dynasty. These caves are generally rectangular, with a front and a back hall linked by a corridor. Their ceilings have the shape of an inverted "U". Thanks to the prosperity of the Silk Road, Dunhuang had a direct pipeline to Chang'an (modern-day Xi'an), the capital of China, both influencing the style of artwork and raising the artistic standards in Dunhuang to unprecedented new levels. The artistic level of the statues and murals in the Mogao Grottos from this period was not inferior

Background Notes on Wu Dai Dang Feng

"Wu Dai Dang Feng" is a term for a Chinese painting style. The pioneer of this technique was Wu Daozi (c. 690-760 A.D.), an artist of the Tang Dynasty. Adept in figure painting, by use of fine, freehand brushwork he skillfully depicted the clothing of his figures as being blown gently in the breeze.

to that of the temples in Chang'an, and examples of nearly all of the influential schools of artwork that existed in Chang'an at that time can by and large be found at the Mogao Grottos. The Sui and Tang Dynasty statues are both more elegant and realistic than those which came before, while the murals show both a greater variety of content and are more masterfully done.

Caves of the Sui Dynasty

The Sui Dynasty reunified the country, ending the warring period of the Southern and Northern Dynasties. China was back on the road of development, becoming a prosperous and powerful country. Emperors of the Sui Dynasty devotedly believed in Buddhism, ordering the large-scale construction of temples and statues throughout the country. During the short 38 years of the Sui Dynasty, more new caves–over one hundred–were constructed in the Mogao Grottos than had been constructed during any previous era.

Caves of the Sui Dynasty are all relatively spacious, with grand statues

Background Notes on Landscapes in Green and Blue
"Landscapes in Green and Blue" was a school of painting which featured outlined-shapes, rich coloring, and strong decorative elements. This style of painting gets its name from the main pigments used, which were mostly made from the minerals azurite (deep blue) and malachite (green). Landscapes of later eras were often ink-wash paintings, which feature more muted color schemes and softer lines.

Mural of dancers, Cave 390, southern wall of the niche

of Buddha that display different characteristics than those of previous eras. Apart from the hall-style cave, which was predominant during the Sui Dynasty, two kinds of caves with central columns were built during that time period. The first was like the central-column style used in previous dynasties, but with new innovations. These caves feature the Trikaya of Buddha–a Buddha flanked by two Bodhisattvas. One Trikaya each stands

Central column, Cave 303

Caisson ceiling, Cave 407

at the front of the central column, and on the southern and northern walls. The main hall has the central column, while the front hall contains statues of Heavenly Kings and demigods, three or four meters high, flanking the entry to the main hall. Eventually, these large statues became the central fixtures of these caves, supplanting the central column in importance. Representative examples of such caves include Caves 292 and 427. Another kind of cave has a square altar under the central column. The central column itself is topped by an inverted pagoda, symbolizing Mount Sumeru. Examples of this kind are Caves 302 and 303.

Sutra Paintings also became popular among murals during the Sui Dynasty. Among the sutras featured in the paintings are *The Vimalakirti Nirdesa Sutra*, *The Western Paradise of Amitabha*, *The Maitreya Sutra*, *The Lotus Sutra*, *The Amitabha Sutra*, and *The Nirvana Sutra*.

Caves of the Sui Dynasty are rife with decorative elements. All the caves are adorned with delicate and gorgeous ornamental patterns. Most caves have caisson ceilings featuring a variety of flamboyant patterns and

Background Notes on Mount Sumeru

Sumeru is a name of mountain in Indian myth. It is said that Mount Sumeru stands 84,000 *yojana* in height (The length of one *yojana* is uncertain: It was the distance an army could march in one day, so estimates range from 9.6 to 24 kilometers). It is surrounded by seven fragrant seas, and then seven gold mountains. Outside the circle of the seventh gold mountain is a salty sea, and this is surrounded by Mount Tiewei. The four continents of the Earth lead from the four directions from Mount Tiewei. In Buddhist cosmology, Mount Sumeru is the center of the universe.

Mural illustrating the reincarnation of Buddha, Cave 397, niche ceiling

designs. The caisson ceiling of Cave 407 is a good example of this trend. The design on the ceiling features a lotus flower with of eight overlapping petals. Inside the lotus flower are three rabbits running in a circle. Each of these rabbits has two ears, but because the rabbits appear to share ears, the painting has only three ears in total, arranged as a triangle in its center. Around the central lotus flower fly eight *apsaras* on a background of sky blue. The caisson is framed by a square border decorated in a design with diamond shapes, followed by two square borders with lotus petals, and finally by a painting of a valances with hanging edges. This decorative work,

Background Notes on Sutra Paintings

In a broad sense, any mural, relief, or sculpture that presents some part of a sutra can be referred to as an illustration of a sutra. In a more narrow sense, the illustration of a sutra refers specifically to an artistic work which shows how the principle ideas of a sutra interrelate.These works usually focus on Buddha, with episodes, scenes, and a multitude of characters from the sutra arranged around him.

Background Notes on the Attendant Bodhisattva

In murals and statues, Buddha is nearly always accompanied by two Bodhisattvas standing on either side known as the Attendant Bodhisattvas. In the case of Amitabha Buddha, these two are Avalokitesvara and Mahasthamaprapta.

The Three Rabbits and Flying Apsaras, incorporates both round and square shapes, symbolizing stillness and dynamics. Full of splendid coloring, this vivid painting is one of the outstanding examples of ancient Chinese art.

Other caisson-ceiling caves of similar note include Cave 305, 314, 397, 401, 403, and 405. Each caisson ceiling has its own distinctive characteristics and creative style, with no two designs alike.

Cave 427

Cave 427 is situated on the upper storey in the middle portion of the Mogao Grottos. The cave has wooden eaves built into the front overhanging the plank path that leads to it. These eaves were renovated during the Song Dynasty, and are only one of four of this kind of wooden structure still extant. Some 28 painted statues can be found in this cave. At the front of the central column, the statue of the Buddha inclines his head as though looking downwards solemnly and compassionately at the creatures of the Earth. His simple cassock and the primitive and solemn palette of colors are all meant to contrast with his deep wisdom. The Bodhisattvas attending him stand on lotus flowers and have gentle smiles on their sedate faces. Their clothing is more flamboyant than that of the Buddha between them. The Bodhisattva on the right wears a coronet,

Background Notes on the Gesture of Bestowing Fearlessness

When Buddha is presented in artistic works, he is often making a gesture (*mudra*) with his hands. A common gesture used in representations of preaching scenes is the Gesture of Bestowing Fearlessness. In this gesture, his right hand is raised with the palm outwards, and his fingers pointed up. This gesture is meant to be one giving reassurance or comfort to the listener.

Thousand Buddhas, Cave 427, western slope of the ceiling

a shirt with short sleeves, aqua ribbons and golden tassels, a brocade skirt with a diamond-shaped patterns, and holds a lotus bud in one hand. The Bodhisattva on the left's coronet has been damaged. He has a reserved expression and is picking up flowers. The gestures and expressions of the statues on the southern and northern walls of the main hall are almost identical to those at the front of the central column.

Compared with the veiled expression of the statues in the main hall, the statues of the Heavenly Kings and the demigods in the front hall are much more explicit in their expressions. On both sides of the door stand *vajra*, demigod warriors who protect the *dharma*. The *vajra* on the right is shouting and drawing back his fist as if preparing for a fight. The muscles of his chest and arms bulge, and his countenance suggests that he is a firm and brave warrior. The *vajra* is barring his teeth and clenching his fists, ready to go into battle. His eyes have a fixed gaze and his muscles are tensed,

Background Notes on the Four Heavenly Kings

The Four Heavenly Kings are guardians protecting the four quarters of Mount Sumeru. Protecting the east is Dhrtarastra, dressed in white and carrying a *pipa*. Protecting the south is Virudhaka, dressed in cyan and grasping a sword. Protecting the west is Virupaksa, dressed in red with a dragon twisted in his hand. Finally, protecting the north is Vaisravana, holding an umbrella in his right hand and a silver mongoose in his left.

making it seem as though he is ready to unleash his power. Two Heavenly Kings stand before each of the western and eastern walls. Together, these are the so-called Caturmaharajakayika, or the Four Heavenly Kings, the guardians of the four quarters of the universe in Buddhist cosmology

The murals in this cave are mostly of the "Thousand Buddhas" and other decorative patterns. The "Thousand Buddhas" are row upon row of miniature Buddhas, about ten to twenty centimeters in height. Each Buddha has its own distinctive color pattern, and they are arranged in such a way to create the effect of colorful, decorative ribbons. On the slopes of the ceiling are patterns of honeysuckle and creeping vines. These stretch and undulate across the ceiling, encircling lotus flowers which have reincarnated children sitting inside them.

Along the upper portion of the walls and corners of the room, *apsaras* fly. Seen from a distance, the long row of flying figures looks like a lace pattern. Up close, one can see that they are almost half-naked. Their long skirts and ribbons float behind them, as though wafting in the breeze. Some hold lotus flowers; others have their palms joining together; while still others carry *konghou*.

Cave 420

Cave 420 is a square hall. On three walls are niches with statues of the Trikaya. At the back of the cave a large niche enshrines a Buddha, two disciples and four Bodhisattvas. The main statue of Buddha wears a cassock and is sitting in the Lotus Position. He has a tender smile on his face, and a solemn and kind expression of compassion. One of the disciples is the oldest of Buddha's followers, Kasyapa, famed for his asceticism. He is covered

Interior of Cave 420

in wrinkles and has exposed ribs in his chest. Another disciple standing close to Buddha is his youngest, Ananda. He has an innocent and artless expression. Ananda was famous for having a perfect memory, and thus was capable of recalling all of the Buddha's sermons. Though Sakyamuni had ten main disciples, most caves contain only the statues of the oldest and youngest disciple, these two representing all of Buddha's disciples. However, Cave 420 contains all ten of the disciples among its statues.

The murals at the tops of the walls illustrate the contents of *The Lotus Sutra*, painted in the form of a scrolling sequence of scenes. On the upper portion of the western wall is a representation of *The Vimalakirti Nirdesa Sutra*. The sutra involves Vimalakirti, a lay minister. Although Vimalakirti never took the tonsure or left home to become a monk, he was well-versed in Buddhism and an eloquent speaker. Countless numbers of people came to debate him on matters of *dharma*, but none could prevail. So many came to hear his wisdom that he often pretended be ill so he could be left alone. Finally, Buddha himself ordered his disciples to visit and debate Vimalakirti. However, none of the ten primary disciples of Buddha dared to go, so Buddha sent Manjusri, considered "the greatest in wisdom", to debate Vimalakirti. Manjusri arrived at Vimalakirti's house with the other disciples and numerous Bodhisattvas following in his train. Naturally, Vimalakirti is viewed as having won the debate. In doing so, he gives the most complete explication of the concept of non-duality, a primary teaching of Mahayana Buddhism.

Background Notes on *Jie Jia Fu* Sitting Position

This is a style of sitting for the purpose of meditation, where the right foot in placed on the left thigh, and the left foot is placed on the right thigh to sit cross-legged. Most of the statues of Buddha in the caves sit in this kind of position.

The portrait of Vimilakirti is on the right side of the niche. He sits on a bench in the center of a hall, carrying an elk-tail whisk in his hand, and arguing with Manjusri. On the other side of the niche opposite to Vimalakirti, Manjusri sits on a lotus-flower pedestal at the center of a hall, raising his hands and arguing with ease. Celestial beings and Bodhisattvas are all positioned to the rear of Manjusri, and the disciples are kneeling around the two men, listening while joining their palm together.

At the Mogao Grottos, paintings of *The Vimalakirti Nirdesa Sutra* continued in popularity long after the Sui Dynasty. Most of these follow the layout depicted here. Other caves with such paintings include Caves 276, 314, 423, and 419.

Distinctive Caves of the Early Tang Period

The Tang Dynasty lasted 290 years. According to the usual practice, it can be divided into four periods: Early Tang, High Tang, Middle Tang and Late Tang.

Background Notes on the Anshi Rebellion

In the fourteenth year of the Tian Bao Era of the Tang Dynasty, An Lushan, a military commissioner of Pinglu and Fanyang, along with his accomplice Shi Siming, rose in revolt against the reign of Tang. Early the next year, he proclaimed himself Emperor Da Yan. The rebellion spanned eight years, which struck at the politics and economy of Tang society heavily and marked the decline of the Tang Dynasty.

Mural of adoring Bodhisattvas, Cave 220, southern wall

In the beginning of the Early Tang Period, the construction of the Mogao Grottos was limited to some extent by a variety of factors. It was not until the reign of Empress Wu Zetian (690–705 A.D.) that the Mogao Grottos began large-scale construction again. However, this construction was unparalleled by any previous era of development at Dunhuang both in scope and innovation.

Most caves during the Early Tang Period were in the style of a hall, with a ceiling like an inverted "U". The main hall was that of a square room, with a niche for the Buddha excavated on the rear wall. No other niches are usually present in these caves. Most caves had an anteroom in the front of the main hall. Connecting these rooms were once wooden hallways covered with decorative paintings. However, with the passing of time, these wooden structures no longer exist.

Cave 96

Amongst the caves of the Early Tang Period, Cave 96 is most prominent. It is located at the southern middle section of the Mogao Grottos, and boasts a giant Maitreya statue standing about 35 meters high. This statue was made in the first year of the Zhengsheng Era (695 A.D.), during the reign of Empress Wu Zetian. As a follower of Buddhism, she wanted to use Buddhism to serve her political ends. When she was about to be enthroned, she had a council of eminent monks proclaim her as the reincarnation of Maitreya Buddha, and ordered a nationwide construction of Maitreya statues.

The outer portion of Cave 96 was originally protected by a wooden structure that was three-stories high, built in the semblance of a temple.

Left: The nine-storied outer structure of Cave 96

Statue of Maitreya, Cave 96

This was reconstructed several times. The existing wooden structure is nine stories in all. It had undergone repairs during the Republic of China, and was completely renovated in 1987. As the tallest wooden structure at the Mogao Grottos, it has become symbolic of the architecture there.

Inside Cave 96, the statue of Maitreya Buddha itself is of stone covered in stucco. The Buddha sits leaned slightly back with his legs stretched in front of him. His eyes look downwards. One hand is raised in the Gesture of Bestowing Fearlessness, and the other stretched out palm down. Because the statue has undergone several reconstructions through its long history, it no longer has its original appearance. However, the body retains the basic features of the Tang Dynasty. This Maitreya statue is one of the largest and greatest of the Buddhist statues in China, rivaling the giant Buddha at the Longmen Grottos in Luoyang, and the Great Buddha in Leshan.

Cave 328

Cave 328 is in the style of a hall, with a ceiling like an inverted "U". The niche inside used to contain a group of nine statues. Now only eight of them remain; the missing one was stolen by an American named Warner in 1924, and is now at the Fogg Art Museum at Harvard University. A statue of Buddha is seated in the middle accompanied by his two disciples, Kasyapa and Ananda, one on each side. The Bodhisattvas flanking these disciples are in relaxed and natural poses. The adoring Bodhisattvas outside the niche are sitting on lotus-flower pedestals. This group of painted statues reflects the artists' expert handling of proportion as well as excellent craftsmanship in presenting fine facial expressions.

Cave 329

While the statues inside the niches of the hall-shaped Cave 329 were reconstructed and substantially altered during the Qing Dynasty, the murals in the cave are original works.

Above the niches on the northern wall is an illustration of *The Maitreya Sutra*. This sutra mainly presents describes Maitreya's future return to Earth to save mankind, and of the wonders of the Pure Land. The upper third of the mural in Cave 329 illustrates Maitreya's ascent to the Pure Land, which is flowing with streams flowing and lotus flowers, with platforms and pavilions erected in-between. Maitreya Bodhisattva sits in the center of a platform preaching to the saints in the twenty-eight heavens. The lower third of the mural shows his descent back to Earth. A table is set at the center, on which seven jewels are laid. Around it, men and women are taking the tonsure to become monks, while bands play celebratory music.

On the southern wall of the cave is an illustration of *The Amitabha Sutra*. This sutra, along with *The Sutra of Contemplating the Buddha of Measureless Life* (also known as *The Meditative Sutra*), and *The Infinite*

Mural illustrating The *Maitreya Sutra*, Cave 329, northern wall

Life Sutra, are the three principle texts of Pure Land Buddhism. With many forms of Buddhism, a person must effectively become a monk in order to have any hope of reaching a higher spiritual state. One innovation of Pure Land Buddhism was to offer ordinary people rituals, mantras, and practices that would help them reach the Pure Land of the West (formerly known as Tusita Heaven), without having to take up the tonsure. Pure Land Buddhism therefore became quite popular during the Tang Dynasty, and many murals at Dunhuang illustrate Pure Land sutras and stories.

Background Notes on the *Shan Jia* Sitting Position

This is one of Buddha's sitting positions. He sits at the center of the seat, his two legs stretching naturally down in parallel with each other, with his feet on a double-lotus-style pedestal. Maitraya Bodhisattva is often in this sitting position.

Flying *apsaras*, Cave 320, southern wall

The Amitabha Sutra illustrates what life in the Pure Land of the West looks like. It is a land where there are no weapons and soldiers, no slavery, no starvation, no plagues, and everyone lives a carefree life. Such a message appealed greatly to people during the Early Tang Period, making murals of *The Amitabha Sutra* quite popular. Of the many murals of this sutra at Mogao, 19 were painted in the Early Tang Period.

The mural in Cave 329 contains seven palatial platforms built over a pond. On each platform are grand halls and pavilions, symbolizing the wonderful world of the Pure Land. Amitabha himself preaches from the Lotus Position at the center of the mural, with a sublime but benevolent expression on his face. He is flanked by his constant companions, the Bodhisattvas Avalokitesvara and Mahasthamaprapta. Other Bodhisattvas wearing coronets and brocade skirts with tassels listen to the sermon. Some

Caisson ceiling, Cave 329

hold their hands prayerfully together with flowers between them, while others lower their heads in contemplation. Dancers and celestial creatures fill the mural. Above them all float drifting clouds, flying *apsaras* and musical instruments.

Matching the Sutra Paintings are four lovely children drawn on either side of the niche on the western wall. They are amusing themselves amongst lotus flowers, pre-occupied with the simple pleasures of life. With their charming naïveté, they remind the viewer of the original simplicity of pure joy.

The four slopes of the ceiling are covered in miniature Buddhas, while the caisson in the center is painted with lotus flowers and flying *apsaras*. At the heart of the caisson is a large lotus with 14 curly petals surrounded by 14 rings of cirrus clouds. Four flying *apsaras* with flowers circle the lotus, their garments flowing in the breeze as they dance among the drifting clouds. The caisson is framed by patterns of coiled grass, interlinked pearls patterns, and a valance. Circling the valance, a group of celestial musicians play *pipa*, *konghou* and waist drums while flying through the sky. The caisson ceiling seamlessly complements the Sutra Paintings. Its rich textures and vivid and dazzling colors make it a masterpiece of decorative paintings from the Tang Dynasty.

Cave 220

Inscriptions inside Cave 220 date it from the sixteenth year of the Zhen Guan Era (642 A.D.), giving the cave great historical value in tracing the development of the Mogao Grottoes. After the Song Dynasty the original walls were covered with stucco and repainted. In the 1940s, these Song Dynasty murals were peeled away, revealing the original works of the Tang Dynasty in perfect condition.

A mural depicting a scene from *The Vimalakirti Nirdesa Sutra* flanks the door on the eastern wall of the cave. This Sutra Painting depicts Manjusri and the various disciples, Bodhisattvas, and celestial beings arriving at Vimalakirti's house for the debate.

Mural illustrating *The Amitabha Sutra*, Cave 220, southern wall

In the sutra, Shariputra, one of Buddha's primary disciples, wondered, "With so many disciples and Bodhisattvas here, where can we all sit?" To solve the seating problem, Vimalakirti invoked the spirit of the Lantern King of Sumeru, and 32,000 lion-shaped seats suddenly appeared.

When lunchtime approached, the disciples of Buddha thought to themselves, "With so many hungry people, where can we find food?" Vimalakirti then teleported himself to the land of Xiangji and brought back an earthen bowl of rice.

On seeing this, some Buddha's disciples whispered, "How can such a little bowl of rice feed so many?" Vimalakirti turned his head and dumped the rice onto the ground. Suddenly, the small amount turned into a mountain of sweet-smelling rice. Everyone then ate to their heart's content.

In the mural, Vimalakirti and Manjusri are on opposite sides of the door. On the southern side, Vimalakirti is seated on his pallet, holding his elk-tail whisk. He has an aroused expression, his eyes sharp and shining, as if debating excitedly. A Bodhisattva is kneeling in front of him holding an earthen bowl. Sitting below them are the princes of various countries. On the northern side of the door, sit Manjusri, Buddha's disciples, Bodhisattvas, as well as emperors and ministers from many countries, each wearing the distinctive clothing of their cultures. All of the onlookers in the mural are respectfully listening to Vimalakirti's teaching.

In the mural, the Chinese emperor majestically stretches out his hands to receive the other kings and emissaries. The scene is strongly evocative of *The Thirteen Emperors* painted by Yan Liben (died 673 A.D.). However, the sense of drama in the mural has a far greater impact than that of Yan's more famous work.

On the southern wall is a mural illustrating *The Amitabha Sutra*. Typical of such paintings, it has a pond in the center, representing the seven

Band of musicians, Cave 220, northern wall

Portrait of Vimalakirti, Cave 220, eastern wall

precious ponds and the water of eight merits described by the sutra. Amitabha Buddha sits in the center on a lotus pedestal, preaching to the multitude of Bodhisattvas around him. He is flanked by his companions, the Bodhisattvas Avalokitesvara and Mahasthamaprapta. Celestial musicians, singers, and dancers surround this scene, drawing our attention to the Buddha. Though the mural is populated with numerous beings, the composition is well-balanced with a harmony between the primary and secondary figures. Even though the palette for the mural is mostly of cyan and green with a limited number of other colors, it nevertheless creates a dazzling and magnificent effect.

Facing this mural on the northern wall is an illustration of *Original Vows of the Medicine-Master Tathagata of Lapis Light*. The seven Bhaisajyaguru Buddhas take center stage in this picture. They are accompanied by eight guiding Bodhisattvas and the twelve yaksha generals, the guardians of the Bhaisajyaguru Buddhas.

This mural is of particular interest because of the light it throws on Tang Dynasty dance and music. In the mural, a concave platform illuminated by many lanterns surrounds a lower pond. On the left of the platform, a group of dancers have poses suggesting powerful, rhythmic movements, like those used in a step dance. On the other hand, the poses of the dancers on the right of the platform suggest grace and elegance. They brandish ribbons in their hands and turn their bodies with ease. Some experts believe that these two dances are the huteng and the *huxuan* dances of the Tang Dynasty. The dancers are accompanied by a singer and band of 27 musicians. Altogether, nearly 20 types of musical instruments are represented in the mural, reflecting the development of music during the Tang Dynasty. These instruments include the zither, panpipe, *fangxiang* (a kind of ancient metallophone), *bili* (an ancient reed instrument made of bamboo), *ruan* (a Chinese lute), waist drum, and the *jiegu* (a large, flat drum).

While ancient Chinese historical records mention the names of different kinds of music and dance, detailed descriptions, explanations, and artistic representations of such are often lacking or incomplete. This mural, along with others at Dunhuang, is a treasure trove of information about the music and dance of the Tang Dynasty. The Silk Road did not just transport silk: Art and culture passed along it as well. Many of the Tang Dynasty musical instruments were introduced to China via the Silk Road. Different dances popular in central China during this era, including the *huxuan*, *huteng* and *tuozhi* dances, were also foreign imports. Since Dunhuang was a choke point on the Silk Road, it is no mystery that the popular music and dance of the time would be depicted on its Tang Dynasty murals. Of just as much interest, the Cache of Manuscripts found at Dunhuang contain musical scores and descriptions of dances from the Tang Dynasty. After years of research, some experts have decoded the musical scores found at Dunhuang, making it possible for us to hear music which had been lost for over 1,000 years.

Cave 57

Some smaller caves were also constructed during the Early Tang Period, one of which is Cave 57. The niche at the back of this hall-style cave has an inner and outer recess. The inner recess contains a Buddha flanked by two disciples and two Bodhisattvas. Originally, the outer recess of the niche contained two Bodhisattvas flanking the inner recess. The sculpting of the statues is rather rigid and lifeless, more in character with that of the Sui Dynasty. However, the painted expressions and garments of the statues are especially vivid and realistic. The murals in the cave include a preaching scene and numerous miniature Buddhas.

The preaching scene depicts Buddha surrounded by disciples, Bodhisattvas and Heavenly Kings. The mural is particularly well-formatted, with the important characters presented full-figure, and the secondary characters standing behind them with often only upper torso and the head visible. Typical of the presentation, the Bodhisattva on the left side is a slender figure, his body and pale face elegantly bent slightly downwards. One hand is raised while the other holds flowers. He wears a coronet on the head and tassels around the neck. The Bodhisattvas behind him are all elegantly painted. The eyes of the Bodhisattvas betray their various inward emotions and characters. Some of the Bodhisattvas are uptight; others, mild-mannered; others, relaxed; and others look as if they are bursting with a secret they long to tell. The overall charm and beauty of the painting leaves many viewers in wonder.

According to historical records from the Tang Dynasty, real-life people were usually used as models for the Bodhisattvas and flying *apsaras*. On one of the murals a monk noted that female models were used to portray

Attendant Bodhisattvas, Cave 57, southern wall

the (male) Bodhisattvas from the Tang Dynasty onwards. The artists wanted to portray the Bodhisattvas of Buddhism as having a natural beauty. Therefore, these images are more realistically painted and somewhat less other-worldly than those which came before.

Magnificent Caves of the High Tang Period

About ten years after the death of Empress Wu Zetian in 705 A.D., during the Kaiyuan Era of Emperor Xuanzong's reign, the flourishing of arts and society known as the High Tang Period began. The High Tang Period spanned about 80 years in the Dunhuang area. During that time, with Silk Road trade at its peak, Dunhuang enjoyed a stable and prosperous society, and people were well-off with ample food and clothing.

During the High Tang Period, Sino-foreign relationships also reached a high point. Along with foreign envoys and merchants, monks traveling west to study Buddhism or east to evangelize often passed through Dunhuang. Economic and cultural exchanges between China and other Asain countries, including India, enriched the culture and art of Dunhuang. Though Buddhism remained pre-eminent in Dunhuang, Daoism, Nestorian Christianity, and Manichaeism were also popular. Under all of these political, economic, and cultural influences, Dunhuang entered its golden era.

More than 100 new caves were constructed during the High Tang

Left: Statue of Buddha, Cave 130

Period. Most of these caves feature a ceiling in the shape of an inverted "U", and a niche on the back wall.

One of the masterpieces of the Tang Dynasty was built in the Mogao Grottos during this period. It is the 26-meter-high statue of Buddha enshrined in Cave 130. This Buddha has a kindly and amiable face with a solemn and dignified bearing. His head and eyes look slightly downwards, conveying a feeling of mildness and benevolence. Since Cave 130 is south of Cave 96, which features the 35-meter-high Maitreya Buddha, this Buddha is called the Southern Giant Buddha.

Cave 45

Cave 45, one of the representatives of the High Tang Period, is situated on the lower story in the middle of the Mogao Grottos. At the back of the cave there is a large niche which has a complete set of seven painted statues. Buddha sits in the center, flanked by his disciples Ananda and Kasyapa, Bodhisattvas and Heavenly Kings. Ananda has his arms clasped before him, a red cassock draped around the shoulders. He is leaning slightly in a relaxed posture with a respectful and cautious demeanor that reveals the virility of youth. The elderly Kasyapa is mature and steady. His kindly looking eyes are full of wisdom. The two Bodhisattvas have tassels around their chests, bands of silk tied over their shoulders, and brocade skirts. Their elegant and refined postures are mirror images of each other. Both have heads slightly cocked at an angle, and half-closed eyes. One hand stretches downwards; the other hand, outwards. Under their bright and smooth skin, you can even sense the flowing of blood. The Heavenly Kings wear armor. Both stand in a heroic pose with one hand on the hip,

Tableau of statues, Cave 45

and the other holding a weapon, their feet treading on evil spirits. These statues are highly realistic and lifelike, since the artists used real people as models. The artists not only worked hard at perfecting their skill at carving and painting the individual statues, but also paid much attention to the look of the tableau as a whole.

Cave 45 features a painting illustrating *The Sutra of Contemplating the Buddha of Measureless Life* on the northern wall. A palace depicts the world of the Pure Land. Buddha sits in the center of this palace, preaching to numerous surrounding Bodhisattvas, with performers playing musical instruments or dancing below.

On the southern wall are some scenes of *Avalokitesvara Bodhisattva* (the Bodhisattva of Compassion, also known as Guanyin or Kannon)

Statue of a Bodhisattva, Cave 45, northern side of the niche

Illustration of the Temple of Treasure Trees, Cave 45, northern wall

rescuing and preaching to people. *The Lotus Sutra* tells in detail some of Avalokitesvara's acts of salvation and compassion toward living beings. One scene represented in this mural is from the story *The Adversity of the Raksa*. The story tells a big ship was voyaging in on the sea. Suddenly, many Raksa–man-eating demons–appeared around the ship. The people on the ship were so frightened that they placed the palms of the hands together and prayed for Avalokitesvara Bodhisattva to protect them. They were thus saved. To the right of this scene is one from "The Adversity of the Bandits". In this story, a caravan of donkeys and merchants were rushed upon by bandits wielding swords. The merchants prayed and were saved. The depictions in the mural is true to life, making it easy for us to imagine the calamities that could happen to those traveling on the Silk Road more than 1,000 years ago. The sutras say that Avalokitesvara Bodhisattva will grant whatever is requested and will save people in any difficulty. Since many people lived in fear of calamity, belief in Avalokitesvara enjoyed a fairly high popularity in China, and many caves at the Mogao Grottos have paintings of scenes involving Avalokitesvara.

Cave 172

Being painted with unrivalled technical skill and having vivid images, mural art at the Mogao Grottos reached its peak of perfection during the High Tang Period. This perfection is exemplified in Cave 172. The two largest murals in the cave both illustrate the same scenes from *The Sutra of Contemplating the Buddha of Measureless Life*. Even though both murals have essentially the same content, the details and compositions of these murals are different enough that they in no way seem repetitive.

The Sutra of Contemplating the Buddha of Measureless Life begins with the story of Bimbisara, the King of Magadha. He was old and had no child, so he asked fortuneteller for help. The fortuneteller told him that a certain Daoist monk living on a mountain would die in future and would be reincarnated as his son. The King was so eager to have a child that he ordered that food be withheld from the monk. And so the monk starved to death.

Nevertheless, no child was born to the King. King Bimbisara went again to the fortuneteller. The fortuneteller explained that Daoist monk had first been reincarnated as a white rabbit. The King then had all of the white rabbits captured. He had them put into prison, and then had nails driven into them until they died. Soon after, his wife, Queen Vaidehi, gave birth to a son, Prince Ajatashatru.

When Prince Ajatashatru became older, the King and Queen took a trip

Mural illustrating the jailing of Queen Vaidehi, Cave 172, northern wall

and left him in charge of the kingdom. While they were away, evil came to Prince Ajatashatru. When his father returned, Ajatashatru had him arrested and ordered that food be withheld from him. Then Ajashatru declared himself King. To save the life of her husband, Queen Vaidehi decided to smuggle food to him. She did this by making a mixture of ghee, honey, and flour, and covering her face with it. On her visit to Bimbisara, he was able to eat this mixture and find sustenance. When Ajatashatru heard what the Queen had done, he decided to kill her. However, two old ministers persuaded him to let her live. Instead, he had her locked up, and then had nails driven into King Bimbisara until he died.

In her grief, Queen Vaidehi prayed to Buddha for comfort. As a result of her earnest prayers, Buddha himself appeared before her. She wanted to know how such an evil thing could have happened. At this point, Buddha explained to her about karma, how good and evil is passed down through reincarnation, and how the moral kernel in each being survives death for further rebirth. Thrilled with this new insight, the Queen begged Buddha to show her how to reach enlightenment. Buddha then explains to her sixteen visualizations that should be contemplated or meditated upon, one after the other. His explanation of these visualizations forms the core teaching of the *The Sutra of Contemplating the Buddha of Measureless Life.*

The two illustrations from this sutra in Cave 172 face each other on the northern and southern walls. Both feature a depiction of the Pure Land of the West in the center. Flanking this depiction, in works done in the style of scroll-paintings, are the story of King Bimbisara and his son on the one side, and scenes from the sixteen visualizations on the other.

Both murals feature performers dancing in worship of Buddha. The painting of the northern wall has two performers in the center, in-between two bands with a total of 16 musicians. From the dancers' poses and the painting style, the mood appears cheerful. The dancing seems rapid and vigorous, with a strong rhythm. The southern wall features a scene with a similar composition, but with different details. Most of the band members in this mural play percussion and wind instruments, so the rhythm of the dance is no doubt strong, and the music clangorous. The dancers themselves also play musical instruments while they dance. One plays a waist drum, and the other plays the *pipa* (a plucked string instrument with a fretted fingerboard) while holding it behind her head. This rather acrobatic way of playing a *pipa* while dancing is often seen portrayed in Tang Dynasty murals. Likely, it was one of the virtuoso dancing skills of the time. In modern times, it has become one of the enduring, representative symbols of Tang Dynasty dance. These paintings are yet another key in understanding the ancient cultural heritage of the Chinese people.

The Sutra Paintings of Cave 172 also give a good illustration of architecture from the Tang Dynasty. Even though China has a long and honored architectural tradition, after hundreds of years of wars and natural catastrophes, most wooden structures from ancient times have either been highly damaged or no longer even exist. Therefore, the only reliable evidence of Tang Dynasty architecture can be found in paintings such as these.

One of the prominent features of traditional Chinese architectures is the emphasis on the beauty of the whole, rather than on individual parts. In a large grouping of structures then, the relationship between the primary and the secondary structures is given the first and highest consideration. This principle is illustrated by the Sutra Painting on the northern wall of the cave. The center of the mural features a bird's-eye view of a magnificent palace. On each side of a vertical axis running through the palace, there is perfect bilaterally symmetry. The different structures in the palace are arranged in the inverted form of the Chinese character 凹 (*ao*), surrounding a large figure of Buddha. There are two palace halls behind the Buddha. The front hall is an elevated pavilion, like those built in Chinese palaces, on the path leading to the main hall. Only the roof of the back, main palace hall can be seen behind the first one. Both halls are connected to corridors leading horizontally to turrets. The turrets themselves have corridors stretching down from them leading to side halls. The main hall at the center is the primary structure, while the side halls are secondary structures and are consequently of smaller stature. Since the side halls are so much smaller than the main hall, to restore a sense of balance to the architecture,

Mural illustrating *The Sutra of Contemplating the Buddha of Measureless Life*, Cave 172, northern wall

near each of the side halls there are small buildings that are elevated a little higher than the side halls. This again forms another relationship between primary and secondary structures.

Architecture is like music. This composition of the main hall and side halls, the corridors and turrets, all of which are contrasted using different heights, gives the palace its rhythm. The delicate and sumptuous style of the individual parts of the palace gives the music color and life. However, the tune itself is conveyed by the purpose of the architecture. Here, the purpose is spiritual. The palace surrounds a central courtyard where religious ceremonies are carried out. In the courtyard are several platforms. The largest platform is in the center of the mural. On it, a large Buddha sits and preaches. Flanking this larger Buddha are two outer platforms, each with a smaller Buddha. The bands and dancers perform in front of the large Buddha in the center on two platforms symmetrically connected with each other. The harmonious coordination of these platforms of different sizes, heights and distances from each other are variations of the main tune.

Overall, this grouping of structures is elegant and magnificent. The predominant feature of the structures is their roofs, which feature gentle slopes, almost totally unadorned by decorations. Their corners are raised slightly and naturally. Each end of their main ridges has ornamental hawk's tails raised skyward. The brackets under their eaves are well-constructed, and the halls under them are spacious. Both the integration of the architecture and the ornamental parts have a graceful and simple style that embodies natural beauty.

Landscape painting of the Tang Dynasty boasts rich coloring, also called "landscapes in green and blue". The technique for painting landscapes in green and blue was lost after the Song Dynasty. However, many paintings in this style are preserved in the murals of the Mogao Grottos. In Cave

172, the Sutra Painting of Manjusri is a typical representative of this style of painting. The mural is a complete landscape scene featuring abrupt mountain peaks, brilliantly rendered in green, blue and reddish-brown. Out from the mountains flows a serpentine stream, embanked on either side by sharp cliffs reminiscent of the magnificent Three Gorges of the Yangtze River. As the stream flows to the foreground, its rushing waves become more apparent. Ultimately, the stream flows into a big river leading out over a vast plain with low hills in the distance. Trees along the banks of the river become smaller and smaller in the distance, and finally disappear.

The artists of this painting exhibited great skill in their use of perspective, contrast, and color, giving the painting a bright and clear atmosphere. While later landscape paintings tended to highlight odd and obscure mountain groups, this painting makes a great effort to reflect realistically the magnificence and grandeur of northern China.

Cave 217

Constructed about 705-707 A.D., Cave 217 is one of the best caves of the Mogao Grottos. The painting on the northern wall illustrates *The Sutra of Contemplating the Buddha of Measureless Life*, while painting on the southern wall illustrates *The Lotus Sutra.*

The painting of *The Sutra of Contemplating the Buddha of Measureless Life* is very similar in composition to those in Cave 172. In the center, there is a palace representing the Pure Land. Scroll-style paintings of the story of King Bimbisara and his son, along with scenes from the sixteen visualizations, are depicted on either side and below the palace. The palace itself is arranged in the inverted form of the Chinese character 凹 (*ao*). In the center,

Interior of Cave 217

Buddha sits on a lotus pedestal expounding doctrine to the surrounding celestial beings and Bodhisattvas. Behind the Buddha is a magnificent and lofty palace hall. On the platform at the front of the Buddha, performers are dancing and playing musical instruments.

The painting illustrating *The Lotus Sutra* on the southern wall has nearly the same format as the mural on the northern wall. In the middle is a small preaching scene. This is surrounded on both sides and below by illustrations of various scenes from the sutra.

The illustration of the parable of the Illusory City to the right of the mural is most striking. In this parable, a group of treasure-seekers are looking for a city with a storehouse of jewels. The trip to the city was so arduous and dangerous that some members of the group wanted to give up and turn back. Their wise leader used his magical powers to create the illusion of the city they were seeking. The travelers entered this city with joy, mistakenly thinking they had arrived. However, after they found rest and encouragement, their leader made the city disappear to ensure that the travelers would continue their journey. Though the city was an illusion, it gave them the strength to go on and find the real city.

To illustrate this scene, a complete landscape was painted on the mural. It is a charming scene, with mountains, a waterfall, streams, and a river zigzagging in the distance. In the center of the mural are some flat hills with many trees and flowers. The travelers are depicted variously as resting by the river while taking in the view or leisurely riding to the Illusory City, which is depicted as a foreign castle. The parable of the Illusory City implies that the road outside the city is desolate and dangerous. However, to make the painting more pleasing to the eye, the artists painted it as a typical landscape in green and blue.

Mural illustrating the chapter of the Universal Door of Avalokitesvara Bodhisattva, from *The Lotus Sutra*, Cave 217, eastern wall

The paintings in Cave 217 were done with a high level of technical skill. The artists showed a mastery of human expressions and body proportions, being especially adept in highlighting fine emotions. There are in total pictures of eight disciples and four Bodhisattvas arranged symmetrically on both sides of the statue of Buddha in the niche. On the south side, the disciple in the front has his right hand raised, as though saying something. He is wearing

Mural illustrating the story of the Illusory City, Cave 217, southern wall

Apsaras flying among pavilions, Cave 217, northern wall

a cassock and has a casual expression. On the north side, the two older disciples have lifelike appearances. The disciple closest to the Buddha has long eyebrows and is looking downwards. The other disciple has his eyes wide open and his mouth slightly agape as if astonished or amazed. The line drawing technique used here gives the murals a powerful, simple and dynamic effect. These are masterpieces of ancient Chinese figure painting. The Bodhisattva painted on the south side of the niche wears a coronet. A long shawl droops down from his shoulder onto the ground, along with his green brocade skirt. His flamboyant style of dress counterpoints his noble posture and expression. Eyes slightly closed, the Bodhisattva stands at attention, two arms overlapping his belly. The artists were particularly good at presenting clothing that looks true to life, making the various textures and qualities of the fabrics seem real.

Cave 148

Apart from Cave 130 (with the Southern Giant Buddha), Cave 148 is the largest cave in size from the High Tang Period. Constructed in 776 A.D., this cave is representative of the late High Tang Period. Like most of the Tang Dynasty caves, it has two halls connected by a corridor. The main hall is rectangular in shape. To the rear of the hall there is a giant statue of Sakyamuni's Nirvana, usually known as the Sleeping Buddha, on a one-meter altar. Since the head of the Buddha is to the south, his right side rests on the altar. There are statues of ten disciples behind the Buddha, but all of these were constructed during the Qing Dynasty. Along with the giant statue of Sakyamuni's Nirvana, there is a Sutra Painting of Nirvana which is one of the largest murals of this theme at Dunhuang.

On the eastern wall, illustrations of *The Sutra of Contemplating the Buddha of Measureless Life* and *The Bhaisajyaguru Sutra* are delicately painted. Buddha preaches in the center of the mural, while saintly beings listen attentively. The many musicians each have a distinctive posture, and the performers dance graciously to the accompaniment of the music. The complicated architectural structures in the mural contain countless twists and turns, palaces and halls, zigzagging corridors and railings, and platforms and waterside pavilions. All appear well-constructed and are harmoniously placed. In a pond of pure water, lotus flowers blossom, birds frolic, and reincarnated children are swimming joyfully. The murals of Cave 148 show off the flamboyant and fine style of High Tang Period art.

Mural illustrating *The Nirvana Sutra*, Cave 148, western wall

Subtle and Elegant Caves of the Middle Tang Period

The Middle Tang Period in Dunhuang is also called the Tufan Period (781-848 A.D.). While the Tang Dynasty experienced a prosperous development, the powerful Empire of Tubo arose in the western regions and Dunhuang came under their sway. Since the Tubo governors actively advocated Buddhism, monks and nuns were ordained in great numbers. At any given time during this period, perhaps more than 1,000 monks and nuns lived in Dunhuang. A number of these monks were of great eminence in the world of Buddhism. The governors excavated or renovated many caves, often putting images of kings inside of them.

During this time, the flamboyant and revolutionary quality of early Tang Dynasty art was gradually superceded by more subtle and elegant tastes. In the realms of literature and art, the artists sought to imbue their art with reserved simplicity. The obvious seeking out of fame and wealth was highly disdained. In painting, vibrant colors fell out of favor as more refined ink-wash paintings gained popularity. The Silk Road was often blocked during this period, isolating Dunhuang from the cultural influences of foreign lands and sometimes even from central China. The artistic climate within Dunhuang became increasingly conservative, and the verve of High Tang Period art with its dazzling and magnificent masterpieces disappeared, even though its basic techniques and styles continued to be imitated. The shift in artistic sensibilities mirrored what was going on in central China to some extent, where well-made compositions, rich variations in line drawings, simple and elegant coloring, and delicate and exquisite depiction of figures were emphasized.

During the Middle Tang Period, more than 50 caves were newly excavated, far less than in the Early Tang and the High Tang Periods. However, the number of paintings per cave was greatly increased, with a single cave having as many as a dozen Sutra Paintings.

In order to include so many paintings, the layout of the murals had to be changed. Generally speaking, the murals of this period have an upper portion which portrays two or three Sutra Paintings, and a lower portion illustrating various chapters of the sutras done in the style of folding-screens paintings. Folding-screen paintings first came into being in the Early Tang Period, but became increasingly popular during the Middle Tang Period. A folding screen is an item of ancient Chinese furniture which stopped the wind and provided shade. After the Northern and Southern Dynasties, families of the literati and officialdom in feudal China usually had folding screens as a part of their residential furnishings. Often these screens had literary works written in calligraphy upon them. From the Tang Dynasty onwards, the use of these screens became popular with common people. The custom of using folding screens in living rooms also affected Buddhist art and became an element of the murals at Mogao. The caves came to be thought of as living rooms. Inside of these caves, common items and things from real life were used to make the caves into spiritual, Buddhist worlds that paralleled the physical world outside.

The more popular themes the Early Tang and the High Tang Periods continued to be used, but a few new sutras were added to the mix. These include *The Diamond Sutra*, *The Redemption from Indebtedness Sutra*, *The Avatamsaka Sutra*, *The Questioning Devas Sutra*, *The Lankavatara Sutra*, and *The Suvarnarabhasa Sutra*. The inclusion of these varied sutras shows the

Statue of the Sleeping Buddha, Cave 158, western wall

Kalavinka birds, Cave 159, northern side of the niche

degree of philosophical ferment present at this time within Buddhist circles. *The Redemption from Indebtedness Sutra* (known in Chinese as *Bao Fumu Enzhong Jing*) is actually a Chinese sutra adapted from the Confucian text, *Canon of Filial Piety*, showing the extent that the Chinese had begun to adapt Buddhism to their own culture and traditions. Images representative of Esoteric (or Tantric) Buddhism were also becoming common. These included many statues of Avalokitesvara in different manifestations, for example, as Amoghapasa ("the Holder of the Infallible Lasso"), as Cintamani-cakra ("Avalokitesvara with a Wish-Fulfilling Wheel"), and as Sahasra-bhuja Sahasra-netra ("Avalokitesvara with a Thousand Hands and Eyes"). Other statues from Esoteric Buddhism, such as Manjusri with a Thousand Hands and Bowls, are also found.

Most caves of Middle Tang Period are hall-style with ceilings in the shape of an inverted "U". The Middle Tang Period inherited the same general style of art work as that of the High Tang Period. Historical records somewhat inaccurately say that the people of the Tang Dynasty adored plump beauty. Actually, this was not consistently true during the entire 300 years of the Tang Dynasty. In Caves 328 and 45, for example, the statues are more shapely. Generally, it was not until the late period of High Tang to Middle Tang that plumpness became a sign of beauty. This can be revealed from the statues in Caves 194 and 159.

Cave 194

Cave 194 is small in scale. The niche in the back of the cave enshrines a tableau of nine statues, which is considered one of the masterpieces of the Middle Tang Period.

The Buddha at the center of the group, bearing a tranquil and benevolent expression, sits with his legs stretched outwards. One of his hands is raised in a preaching gesture, while the other hand is on his lap. On the right is a statue of Kasyapa with a beaming face and devout posture, wrapped in a cassock. His hands joined at the palms in a greeting. Opposite him is a statue of Ananda. The carefree youth, innocent and naive, has his two hands overlapping his belly.

The statue of the Bodhisattva standing next to Kasyapa is wrapped in brocade silk with his skirt touching the ground. He stands barefoot on a lotus pedestal, leaning back a little in a charming posture. He has a gentle smile on his white-skinned face. The southern Bodhisattva has a plump figure, smooth and bright skin, and a double-coiled bun on the head. Looking downwards, he also bears a slight smile. He is wearing a luxuriant sleeveless garment, with a round collar and a piece of silk draped over his left elbow. His clothes hang gracefully and easily from his body, and have realistic decorations.

To the north, the statue of the Heavenly King wears a helmet and armor, and bears a sword in his right hand. Looking robust and mighty, he leans forwards with his weight on his right foot with a look of firm

Statue of a heavenly king, Cave 194, northern side of the niche

Statue of a heavenly king and a Bodhisattva, Cave 194, southern side of the niche

determination. The Heavenly King opposite him has a high wispy bun. He also wears wearing armor, but smiles brightly. Normally, the images of the Heavenly Kings in past dynasties gave glowering looks. However, this statue is far from a traditional image. Instead, he looks affable and kind, like a normal person. Evidently, he is supposed to be the image of an open-minded and generous general.

Flanking the niche are demigods. Both statues are naked above the waists. The artists highlighted their strong muscles, swelling veins, and round eyes, showing them as a display of strength and power from head to foot. The northern demigod smiles while shaking his fist. The southern demigod wears a war-skirt and looks as if he is holding his breath before going to battle. The artists carved the statue to convey the moment just before the demigod was about to strike, perhaps with the power of a thunderbolt.

Cave 159

Similar in layout and artistic style to Cave 194, Cave 159 has a niche in its back wall which originally housed a set of seven statues. However, the central statue of Buddha no longer exists, leaving only statues of two disciples, two Bodhisattvas, and two Heavenly Kings.

The Bodhisattva on the right has a fair complexion and is looking down. His upper torso is naked, and he wears an embroidered skirt. His plump figure is natural and graceful. The elegant Bodhisattva on the left has arched eyebrows and round cheeks. He wears his hair in a high, wispy bun, and has a gorgeous costume. The outer two statues of Heavenly Kings both have glowering looks. Their eyes stare forward, and their fists

Mural of the Tubo king and attendants, Cave 159, eastern wall

are clenched as if ready to fight. The forceful images of the Heavenly Kings provide a strong contrast with the peaceful Bodhisattvas.

To the left of the niche are Sutra Paintings of Manjusri Bodhisattva, and to the right, Sutra Paintings of Samantabhadra Bodhisattva. Both are delicately executed. In the Sutra Painting of Manjusri, Manjusri Bodhisattva bears a tranquil and kind expression. He holds a wish-fulfilling pearl while sitting on a lion throne, and is surrounded by the Eight Groups of Demigods and Semi-devils and other celestial figures, dynamically posed. The flying apsara to the rear of the lion stretches her head forward artlessly and innocently, while the lower one looks downwards as if in contemplation. The one who is trying hard to pull the lion has his eyes wide open.

The three celestial musicians are of the most vivid images. The one in front plays the fife. Her face is inclined, looking downwards, as if moving her head with the music. The one in back keeps rhythm. She smiles brightly, obviously in a good mood. The middle one plays the bamboo flute attentively, her eyes watching her fingers. She stands barefoot on a lotus pedestal, with raised toes as if tapping her feet.

The southern wall of the cave has paintings illustrating the *The Maitreya Sutra*, *The Sutra of Contemplating the Buddha of Measureless Life*, and *The Lotus Sutra*, while the northern wall has paintings illustrating *The Questioning Devas Sutra*, *The Bhaisajyaguru Sutra*, and

Background Notes on the Eight Groups of Demigods and Semi-devils

These different groups of spirits are considered to be protectors of the Buddha dharma: Deva, Naaga, Yaksa, Gandharva, Asura, Garuda, Kimnara and Mahoraga. Among these, the Deva and Naaga usually take the set of honor. In art work, a depiction of members these two groups is thus seen as representative of the entire eight groups.

Left: Celestial musicians, Cave 159, northern side of the niche

The Avatamsaka Sutra. On both sides of the door of the eastern wall are paintings illustrating *The Vimalakirti Nirdesa Sutra*. Beneath the Sutra Paintings are folding-screen paintings.

The painting illustrating *The Vimalakirti Nirdesa Sutra* has a striking portrait of the Tubo king. Images of the kings of various nations were usually portrayed in paintings of *The Vimalakirti Nirdesa Sutra*. In this mural, the Tubo king takes the lead. Tall and dignified, he stands on a square platform in Tubo garb with an umbrella held over his head. His outer robe, with its large lapels and sleeves, wraps around an under-tunic with a V-neck, and is held on by a leather belt. He carries a dagger, and exhibits a pious and devout expression. This painting reflects how contents of the various murals were subtly changed during the Tubo Era to emphasize and heighten the importance of the Tubo people by including adoring portraits of the Tubo kings.

While the artistic level of the figure paintings in this cave is not inferior to those of the Early Tang and the High Tang Periods, the artists had more elegant and simple tastes, abjuring the use of strong and flamboyant colors.

Cave 158

Cave 158, a large-scale cave, features a nearly identical layout as the High Tang Cave 148, and like Cave 148 features a giant statue of Sakyamuni's Nirvana, or Sleeping Buddha. The 15 meter-long statue, a magnificent example of Chinese art, sleeps quietly with half-closed eyes, and head resting on his right hand and a pillow. His expression is peaceful, almost smiling, like that of a dozing girl, as his facial features and wispy bun

Interior of Cave 158

Grieving disciples, Cave 158, southern wall

Grieving kings, Cave 158, northern wall

are all carved in bright, clean lines. The cassock is draped naturally in lengths of soft folds, capturing the underlying curves of the body quite well. Flanking the Sleeping Buddha are statues representing the Buddha of the past, and the Buddha of the future.

The murals of the cave, all depicting scenes related to Nirvana that echo the theme of the Sleeping Buddha, are also masterpieces of the Middle Tang Period. Bodhisattvas are painted behind the Sleeping Buddha. These all feature peaceful expressions, seemingly without emotion or concern with the mundane problems or desires of daily, as if they have all reached a high level of spirituality and possess a transcendent understanding of Nirvana.

The northern wall has an adoring scene of the Four Heavenly Kings, along with the Eight Groups of Demigods and Semi-devils and other celestial beings, heading to the city of Kusinagara, where Sakyamuni Buddha died and was therefore translated into Nirvana. The flying *apsaras* above all carry tassels, and are falling softly to Earth from rose-colored clouds. In the other caves at the Mogao Grottos, the flying *apsaras* are all full of joy and pleasure. However, the *apsaras* in this painting, though still swathed in festive ribbons, all have slightly knitted the brows and look somehow sad.

On the left, kings and princes of various countries and ethnic groups in the western regions are mourning in their own distinctive ways. In a tragic scene, some are piercing their own bellies; some, stabbing their own chests; others, mutilating their own noses or ears. On the right, the Chinese emperor is portrayed wearing a crown with tassels. He is crying. However, compared with his counterparts from other ethnic groups, his expression is far more subdued, perhaps due to the influence of Confucianism. The portrayal of the different cultures and their modes of extreme mourning reflect the artists' understanding of real life.

The southern wall also portrays a scene of grief. There are not as many figures in this picture, but the scene is more dramatic and touching. In the center of the mural, Kasyapa, one of the main disciples of Buddha, has just come down from the mountain after seeing Buddha's death and his attainment of Nirvana. In deep mourning, he is crying with his hands raised in intense sorrow. The other disciples are trying hard to console him. Another disciple, Ananda is kneeling down on the ground in deep sorrow, as though he has been crying for quite a long time. He props himself up with one hand, while cupping the other hand over his ear, as though he is still trying to listen to Buddha preach.

Generally speaking, the murals in Cave 158 are simple, yet profound. Instead of describing *The Nirvana Sutra* in detail, it is simplified and all superfluous elements are omitted, thereby highlighting the main theme of the grief of the disciples over Buddha's death. In order to create a lifelike and realistic tableau, great importance was attached to the posing and expressions of the individual figures in the painting.

Children playing, Cave 112, western wall

Interior of Cave 112

Cave 112

Cave 112 is a small cave, famous for its elegant and exquisite portraits. A good example of this can be found in the illustration of *The Sutra of Contemplating the Buddha of Measureless Life*. The upper portion of the mural has several halls symbolizing celestial palaces and pavilions. Buddha preaches in the center, faced on both sides by Bodhisattvas listening to his sermon intently. Dancers with their musical accompaniment are portrayed below the Buddha. The central dancer, full of dynamic beauty, is all-but nude above the waist save for her necklace. She plays a *pipa* behind her head, and is lifting up one foot as though in the midst of jumping through the air, while ribbons swirl around her. Forming a harmonious scene, six musicians surround the central dancer,

Right: Dancer playing a *pipa* behind her head, Cave 112, southern wall

playing the *pipa*, the *ruan*, the *konghou*, clappers, fife, and *jilougu* (a small drum).

The painting illustrating *The Redemption from Indebtedness Sutra* on the northern wall also has a dancer, performing robustly and vigorously with hand motions and jumps and stepping. Eight musicians surround her, playing the *zheng* (a Chinese zither with 25 strings), *pipa*, the *sheng* (a Chinese reed pipe), clappers, fife, waist drum, *jiegu*, and the *jilougu*. Most of the musical instruments in this band are percussion instruments, indicating that the music was very rhythmical. From these images of dancers and musicians, we can well imagine the development of Chinese music and dance some 1000 years ago.

The Splendid Rebirth of the Mogao Grottos in the Late Tang Period

In 848 A.D., Zhang Yichao, a native of Dunhuang, took over as a leader of the Guiyi ("Uprising") Army, overthrowing the occupying Tubo army. Three years later, Zhang Yichao's army was recognized by the Tang central government. Accordingly, he was given official appointment over the army as its commander in chief. He took control over the Hexi Corridor, putting in place a land-sharing system that attached great importance to

The Mogao Grottos in autumn

the agricultural development in order to heal the war-torn province. The Silk Road was again opened for traffic, and so Dunhuang consequently experienced another spurt of prosperity.

During this time, the artist at Dunhuang wanted to bring back the grand spectacle of High Tang Period art and its dazzling murals. The caves of the Late Tang Period are therefore stylistically rich. Most are halls with a ceiling in the shape of an inverted "U", and a niche excavated on the western wall. However, some caves were actually built off the corridors of older caves, and thus are situated on a north-south axis, with entryways and niches oriented accordingly. A new style of cave also appeared, with a carved Buddha set in the center of the cave on an altar. Behind the Buddha, a screen runs clear to the ceiling of the cave.

Statue of a Bodhisattva, Cave 196, northern side of the altar

Cave 196

Dug in 892–893 A.D., Cave 196 is one of the most important caves of the Late Tang Period. The cave was constructed at the highest point of the southern cliff. Protecting the front of the cave is part of the original wooden superstructure, with four octagon-shape poles support its thick crossbeams. This is the oldest extant wooden structure at the Mogao Grottos.

The main hall is a square hall with a depth of about 10 meters. It has a horseshoe-shaped altar at the center, behind which a screen stretches to the ceiling. Most of the statues on the altar are two to three meters in height. Representing one of most vividly painted statues in this cave, in the center of the group a 2.74-meter-tall statue of Buddha sits tranquilly in the Lotus Position, while disciples respectfully and solemnly accompany him on both sides. He bears a thoughtful expression with his eyes half-closed. Naked from the waist, he is wrapped in silk.

A monk brushing his teeth, Cave 196, western wall

Many Sutra Paintings are painted on the walls of Cave 196, one of which illustrates the fight between Sariputra and Raudraska. In the story, Sudatta, a government minister in the country of Sravasti, wanted to build a *vihara* (a kind of monastery) and ask Sakyamuni to come there and preach. To comply with Sudatta's request, Sariputra, one of the Buddha's main disciples, arrived in Sravarti first and purchased a garden owned by the local prince upon which to build the vihara. However, the people of Sravasti believed in Raudraska, a certain non-Buddhist who represented six other teachers of heretical schools. They strongly opposed Sakyamuni's upcoming visit when they got wind of the plans.

To settle the conflict, a public duel of supernatural power was thus arranged between Raudraska, the disciple of heresy, and Sariputra. Raudraska supernaturally transformed himself into a mountain. Correspondingly, Sariputra transformed into a powerful *vajra* warrior and smashed the mountain. Next, Raudraska transformed himself into a buffalo. Sariputra became a lion and mauled the buffalo to death. Then, Raudraska changed into a pond. Sariputra turned into an elephant and sucked up all of the water in the pond. When Raudraska became a poisonous dragon, Sariputra in the form of a golden bird came and pecked the poisonous dragon to death. Finally, Raudraksa transformed himself into a huge tree. Sariputra transformed himself into King Vaisravana and cut the tree down. After cutting down the tree, Sariputra created a hurricane and blew Raudaksa away. Rauduka then admitted defeat. He and the six heretical teachers he represented were then all compelled to convert to Buddhism.

In the mural, Sariputra calmly sits on the left on a high lotus pedestal, flanked by disciples of Buddha. Rauduka sits on a high pedestal on the right, accompanied by the six heretical teachers. Even though all six rounds of the battle are depicted, the mural focuses on the strong hurricane. Rauduka sits on his pedestal, startled and panicked because a huge tree is falling down upon him. As his high pedestal sways dangerously in the wind, some of the heretics are erecting long ladders to rescue him, while others are futilely trying to steady the pedestal with ropes. The contrast between the calm on the Sariputra side and the chaos on the enemy side represents the fight between good and evil.

The depictions of the six heretical teachers are exaggerated humorously by the artists. For example, in the mural, after the heretics are forced to take the Buddhist tonsure, some of them touch their bare heads in shame, while others wash their heads. Some of the heretics try on their cassocks in great curiosity, while still others point at each other's bare heads in mirth. The whole picture is one of ease and humor.

Cave 156

Zhang Huaishen, Chief Commander of the Guiyi Army, constructed Cave 156 in commemoration of the retaking of the Hexi Corridor. An eight-meter-long painting of Zhang Yichao parading with his troops occupies the lower half of the south wall. Painted as a long, horizontal scroll, the picture starts in the west with a vanguard of soldiers blowing horns, beating gongs and drums, carrying flags, and holding weapons. These are followed by performers dancing and singing. A majestic-looking Zhang Yichao is portrayed in the center of the mural, wearing red clothes and riding a horse. The rest of his army and soldiers carrying the supplies follow him. The picture, vividly and realistically reflecting a local commander in full parade, boasts an air of magnificence and joy.

At the bottom of the northern and eastern walls is a painting of Lady Song, Zhang Yichao's wife, who was given the honorary title Madam Song of Henei County. In this picture, acrobats, dancers and musicians take the lead, followed by carriages, maids of honor, couriers, and sedan chairs.

Zhang Yichao in full military parade, Cave 156, southern wall

Zhang Yichao in full military parade (detail), Cave 156

Behind these Madam Song, escorted by eight imperial bodyguards, comes riding a white horse. She has a high wispy bun, richly decorated with flower-shaped hairpins. She wears a long skirt, and is wrapped in light clothing. Behind her is a bevy of attendants. Taking up the rear are hunters, camels, and horses carrying supplies.

These two paintings, featuring Zhang Yichao and his wife on their travels, exhibit the fine artistic heritage of the High Tang Period, restoring the grand and magnificent atmosphere, the flamboyant coloring, the fine brushwork, and the variety of figures. Their naturalistic style, having content directly drawn from real life, demonstrates yet another element of what constitutes traditional art at the Mogao Grottos.

Caves 16 and 17

Cave 16 is a large-scale cave constructed by Hong Bian, an eminent monk who lived in the Late Tang Period. Unfortunately, all the statues inside have been damaged, and the extant murals inside the cave were all repainted in later dynasties, displaying none of the characteristics Tang Dynasty style art. Built into the north of the corridor inside Cave 16 is

Statue of a monk in meditation, Cave 17

another small cave, Cave 17. Cave 17 is important because a number of rolls of ancient Buddhist manuscripts were unearthed there in the year 1900. It is therefore known as "the Cache of Manuscripts Cave". The cave was originally built as a memorial for Hong Bian, and so contains a life-size statue of Hong Bian inside. Wearing a cassock, he has a solemn bearing, being the depiction of a wise, old monk of great eminence. The realistically carved statue of Hong Bian reflects the advanced level of sculpture from that time. The mural behind the statue depicts two big trees, and the images of a nun and a maid of honor. The characteristic plump faces of the two reflect the aesthetic values of the Tang Dynasty. The refined and smooth lines, as well as the gentle and graceful rendering of the figures, is of a fairly high artistic level. This mural is an excellent work from the Late Tang Period.

A maid of honor, Cave 17, northern wall

Sunset of the Desert

Five Dynasties through the Yuan Dynasty

Lacking cultural support from central China, Dunhuang became an isolated island of culture. Although it still experienced the continual construction of new caves, the artistic level declined day-by-day. The reunification of China under the Yuan Dynasty brought a brand-new look to the caves of Dunhuang. However, only a small number of caves were newly dug during this time, making this creation of new art just a flash in the pan.

Panorama of the Mogao Grottos and the location of the caves from the Five Dynasties through the Yuan Dynasty

The last phase of Dunhuang art generally ran from the Five Dynasties Period through the Yuan Dynasty (10th–14th centuries). At the decline of the Tang Dynasty, the Cao family replaced the Zhang family and took over command of the Guiyi Army. At this time, exchanges between Dunhuang and central China were almost cut off because Dunhaung was surrounded by local Huihu kingdoms to both the east and the west. Lacking cultural support from central China, Dunhuang became an isolated island of culture. Although Dunhuang still experienced a continual construction of new caves, the artistic level declined day-by-day.

Beginning in the early half of the 11th century, the Western Xia ruled Dunhuang for around 200 years. The Western Xia Dynasty had a policy of forcefully conquering its neighbors. The continual warfare brought cultural development to a crawl in Dunhuang. During the late Western Xia Dynasty, some cultural elements from central China began reappearing in the cave art. The reunification of China under the Yuan Dynasty brought a brand-new look to the caves of Dunhuang. However, only a small number of caves were newly dug during this time, making this creation of new art just a flash in the pan.

The Arrival of Clan-Style Caves

During the Five Dynasties and the Song Dynasty, Dunhuang was governed by the Cao family (941–1036 A.D.). The Cao family regarded

Interior of Cave 61

Buddhism as a means to ensure stability of their governance, and so constructed some 55 new caves in the Mogao Grottos. Many of the caves from past dynasties were also renovated, and most of the extant large-scale caves of the Mogao Grottos date from this period. In conjunction with their work on the caves, the Cao family set up an art academy, like those found in central China, to cultivate artisans engaged in carving and painting statues, and in painting murals. This academy was in charge of the construction of temples, monasteries, and caves in the Dunhuang region. Despite having an art academy, most of the art work produced was in imitation of that which had come before.

Statue of a Heavenly King, Cave 55, southern side of the altar

Most of the murals of this period were Sutra Paintings that had the same basic style and content as those of previous periods. There were a few innovations during this period. For example, expanding upon a trend begun during the rule of the Zhang family, a growing number of donor portraits in the murals are especially large in scale. Previously, such figures were relatively small so as not to detract from the portraits of Buddha or various Bodhisattvas. While there were a small number of innovations, cultural developments in central China had almost no influence in Dunhuang owing to its isolation. Eventually, this resulted in a stultifying rigidity in the Cao art academy. With an increasing tendency towards serious formalization, art in the Mogao Grottos inevitably waned.

Cave 98

Cave 98, one of the larger caves of the Mogao Grottos, is a rectangular hall, about 15 meters in width, and 20 meters in height, with a ceiling in the shape an inverted "U". It has an altar in the center of the cave, with a back screen reaching to the ceiling. In an innovation from the Five Dynasties Period, the four corners of the ceiling have shallow niches, on which images of the Four Heavenly Kings are portrayed, reflecting the builder's desire for peace and protection stretching to the four corners of the universe. The cave has eleven Sutra Paintings in total, most of which appear similar both in content and style to previous murals.

Offering a crucial historical record, a large number of donor portraits

Background Notes on the Techniques of Plastering and Gilding

According to folklore in Dunhuang, the craftsmen made the murals by mixing plaster of Paris with some glue. They put this mixture in a waterproof leather bag. The mouth of the bag would have a slim tube connected to it. When the artists wanted to use some plaster, they just needed to squeeze the leather bag and apply it to the wall. They would then smooth out the plaster to draw or paint on it. Gilding was one technique used in mural paintings to add color. When the plaster was dried completely, the places where they wanted to apply gold were smeared with some extra glue, and then gold foil would be applied. It would stick only to the places where the glue was applied, forming raised lines of gold on the mural.

Mural depicting the Heavenly King of the East, Cave 98, ceiling

Donor portrait of the Huihu princesses, Cave 98, eastern wall

were painted in Cave 98. On the southern wall of the corridor contains portraits of the cave's builder, CaoYijin, and his sons. Portraits of female members of the Cao family occupy parts of the eastern and northern walls. The Cao family was associated with the Zhang and Suo families through marriage. Therefore, the images of Zhang Yichao and Suo Xun, two historically renowned figures of Dunhuang, appear on the northern wall. All of these portraits are quite large. For example, the portrait of Cao Yijin is 2.42 meters in height.

In order to stabilize the regime, the Cao family also married into the

Donor portrait of Li Shengtian, King of Yutian, Cave 98, southern side of the eastern wall

family of the King of Yutian (modern-day Hetian, Xinjiang).This is reflected in Cave 98 by adoring portraits of the King and Queen of Yutian on the eastern and southern walls. The King of Yutian stands 2.82 meter in height, and wears a dragon robe and a crown on his head. He bears a pious and holy appearance. His portrait is labeled with the inscription, "Sage Son of Heaven of the wealthy country of Yutian". Madam Cao, the Queen of Yutian stands behind him. Other female donors are gorgeously dressed in Huihu or Han costumes.

Cave 61

Built in 947–951 A.D., Cave 61 is often called the "Hall of Manjusri" because Manjusri Bodhisattva is enshrined inside. There cave contains twelve murals of various sutras. In particular, a mural illustrating *The Abhiniskramana Sutra* stands out. Done in the style of a folding-screen painting, its 33 consecutive panels show in detail the entire life of Sakyamuni, from birth, through his teaching, and then on to Nirvana. This mural contains one of the most detailed depictions in the world of Buddha's life.

Naturally, much of the art work in the cave is devoted to Manjusri. Since the time of the Northern Dynasties, Manjusri has been a popular figure in Chinese Buddhism. *The Avatamsaka Sutra* records that Clear and Cool Mountain (Qingliang Shan) was the home of Manjusri. Chinese Buddhists believe that Mount Wutai in Shanxi Province is the Clear and Cool Mountain, giving Mount Wutai an important place in Chinese liturgy. A 13.45-meter long and 3.42-meter high mural of Mount Wutai is depicted on the western wall of Cave 61. The mural

Donor portrait of the Queen of Yutian, Cave 61, northern side of the eastern wall

Mural of Mount Wutai, Cave 61, western wall

depicts a panorama of mountains, plains, cities, monasteries and temples of various sizes, from an area stretching 250 kilometers from ancient Zhenzhou (modern-day Zhengding County, Hebei Province) to the city of Taiyuan, Shanxi Province. The painting contains over 47 monasteries, 17 *aranyas* (small Buddhist temples or retreats, usually located in forests or on mountains) and 21 nunneries. These, along with the cities, bridges and other structures in the mural, form a precious record for the study of ancient architecture. In 1973, Liang Sicheng, a well-known expert of ancient Chinese architecture, led a team to Mount Wutai and found the long-lost main hall of Foguang Temple, by using this mural for reference.

Stories of eminent monks related to Mount Wutai are depicted in the

Mural of traveling merchants, Cave 61, western wall

picture, as well. These include Fotuoboli (佛陀波利), Jietuo (解脱), Fazhao (法照), and Xianglong (降龙和尚), all historic monks recorded in ancient literature. A representative example of these monks would be Fotuoboli. Originally from India, Fotuoboli first came to Mount Wutai in 676 A.D. It is recorded that Manjusri Boddhisattva appeared to him as an old man and said to him, "If you want to encourage the true practice of Buddhism, why don't you bring *The Dharani of the Jubilant Corona* back from India? This sutra will be very helpful to Chinese Buddhist monks."

In the year 683 A.D., the monk Fotuoboli returned to China, presenting *The Dharani of the Jubilant Corona* to the Emperor in Chang'an. In return, the Emperor gave him a reward of silk, then ordered

Interior of Cave 55

someone to translate the sutra and give the original back to him. The monk Fotuoboli went on to Mount Wutai, and became a hermit living in the *vajra* cave. Two scenes of Fotuoboli at Mount Wutai are depicted in the picture.

A vast panorama of the society of the time is also shown in the picture. There are many people involved in varied daily activities, including traveling, meditating, pulling camels or donkeys, husking rice, and presenting offerings. The kinds of people include men of nobility, officials, common people, businesspeople, woodsmen, prisoners, and rulers. From this mural, we can imagine in our minds ancient social life.

Caves of the Western Xia Dynasty

In 1038 A.D., a member of the Dangxiang branch of the Qiang ethnic minority group, Li Yuanhao, established the Western Xia Dynasty, which ruled Dunhuang for a total of 191 years. This was the longest governing ethnic minority regime ruling Dunhuang since its founding. Dozens of new caves were created during the Western Xia Dynasty, but the majority of these were actually renovations of older caves. Renovations included repainting old murals. Western Xia artists preferred using green pigments (made of malachite) with highlights of gold, creating a splendid sparkling effect inside the caves.

Caves 16 and 130

Cave 16 is a large cave first excavated during the Late Tang Period. However, it underwent thorough renovation during Western Xia Dynasty. The corridor leading to the main hall has preaching scenes painted on the upper portions of its two walls, and adoring Bodhisattvas on the lower portion. Although these Bodhisattvas are well-proportioned and have intricately painting costumes, their dull expressions and stiff bodies cause them to lack vitality.

Inside the hall itself, the four walls are painted with miniature Buddhas. The vermillion caisson on the ceiling bears a phoenix at the center of a lotus flower. At the four corners of the caisson are four golden dragons which seem dazzling on the red background. Checkerboard and floral patterns cover the four slopes of the ceiling.

Cave 130 features a flamboyantly colored caisson like that of Cave 16. It has a golden-dragon pattern at the four corners of the caisson. Surrounding the caisson and going down the four slopes of the ceiling are square frames of decorative and geometric patterns, such as chains of pearls, squares, checkerboards, all elements of Western Xia ornamental art.

Cave 97

Cave 97 is another cave renovated during the Western Xia Dynasty. Like Caves 16 and 130, its caisson ceiling is also decorated with dragon patterns. However, it differs from most caves at Mogao because the Sixteen Arhats are depicted therein. In Buddhism, an Arhat is one who has attained enlightenment and is no longer subject to the law of death and rebirth.

While Theravada Buddhism worships the Sixteen Arhats as examples we should all aspire to follow, Mahayana Buddhism focuses on Bodhisattvas. Though a Bodhisattva is by nature only someone who has not yet obtained full enlightenment, Mayahana Buddhism generally adds to this teaching the idea that the Bodhisattvas are people who could enter Nirvana (and become Arhats), but out of compassion choose not to in order to stay behind and help others. Consequently, most of the art work at Mogao celebrates Boddhisattvas, and Arhats are rarely portrayed there.

Two rows of six Arhats each are painted facing each other on the southern and northern walls, and four more are painted on the eastern wall. As these are meant to be portraits rather than generic representations, each Arhat is given his own individual character. For example, the Arhat in the upper mid-section of the northern wall has big eyes and a beetle brow. He sits on a rock, with a cassock wrapped around his naked shoulders. His left hand is on his lap, while his right hand has a raised hammer. Beneath the rock where he is sitting, there is a stream. On the hill on the other bank of the stream,

An Arhat, Cave 97, northern wall

a mysterious bowl sends out marvelous shafts of light. The first Arhat on the northern wall sits in the Lotus Position with his palms together, and an affable expression on his face, while the ninth Arhat on the southern wall is an old Buddhist monk. Since he is so old and shaky, he sits on a rock flanked by his servants, holding his crutch with both hands. A young monk with his palms together in greeting is turning back to stare at the old monk.

The upper portion of the cave niche was painted with distinctive, child *apsaras* flying in the air. Their crowns are partially shaved, leaving pigtails sprouting from both sides of the head. They are wearing shirts with floral patterns, red ribbons around the waist, and red boots. Like nearly all *apsaras* at Mogao, scarves and ribbons float through the air around them. The clothes, appearances, and hairstyles all depict characteristics of the Qiang ethnic minority group.

Cave 61

While the main hall of Cave 61 still maintains the character of its original construction during the Five Dynasties Period, the corridor leading to the hall was renovated during the Western Xia Dynasty. The walls of the corridor contain murals related to Tejaprabha Buddha (Buddha of blazing lights), based on the sutra, *Prajvalonisa Vjrabhairava Padvinasa-sri-dharani*. In one illustration, Tejaprabha Buddha sits on a wheeled-carriage with a gold dharma wheel balanced on one finger. Revealing the astrological beliefs of people long ago, Tejaprabha is followed nine astronomical bodies: Mercury, Venus, Mars, Jupiter, Saturn, the Sun, the Moon, and Rahu and Ketu (two invisible planets in Indian astrology). In Buddhism, astronomical bodies were considered supernatural beings and hence were depicted as deities.

Tejaprabha Buddha, Cave 61, southern wall of the corridor

For example, in the mural, Venus is shown as a female deity playing a *pipa*; Mars is drawn as a heavenly king wearing a donkey-like crown, and carrying a bow in one hand and chains in the other; the Moon is represented as a female deity wearing a bird-like crown, and holding a moon-wheel. Above these deities are the twelve houses of the zodiac, and representations of 28 constellations. The images in the mural reflect the Buddhist understanding of astronomy and nature.

Apart from those at the Mogao Grottos, illustrations of Tejaprabha Buddha have been unearthed in the Ningxia area and elsewhere in western China, illustrating the prevailing belief in Tejaprabha Buddha during the Western Xia Dynasty.

Portraits of ten donors are preserved to the left of the Tejaprabha

Buddha on the northern wall; while the southern wall contains the portrait of a slightly hunchbacked nun, who is holding flowers between palms clasped piously together. The artists placed explanatory labels beside the portraits in the corridor. These inscriptions, written in Chinese characters and the script of the Western Xia, provide a valuable reference for the study of the art and the history of the Western Xia Dynasty.

The Dunhuang Caves during the Yuan Dynasty

The Western Xia Dynasty ended in 1227 A.D. when the Hexi Corridor was occupied by the Mongolian Yuan Dynasty. With Yuan rule, gradually the region was opened up again to other parts of China, and many farmers immigrated there to cultivate the land. By the early 14th century, traffic between the east and the west was booming once again, with merchants

Background Notes on Vajrayana Buddhism

Vajrayana Buddhism is a major school of Buddhism, which began to gain popularity in India in the 7th century. Early in the 8th century, it was introduced to China. The hallmarks of Vajrayana Buddhism include the recitation of the mantras, the use if *mudras* (hand gestures which have special meaning or power), and contemplation as a way to enlightenment. In the early 9th century, a Japanese monk named Kukai came to learn Buddhism in China. When he introduced Vajrayana Buddhism to Japan, it became the basis for the Shingon sect. From the 8th century to the 11th centuries, Vajrayana Buddhism was gradually introduced to Tibet, syncretizing with local Tibetan Buddhism, and forming Zangmi, which is the Tibetan sect of Buddhism.

Interior of Cave 465

Donor portrait, Cave 465, eastern wall

traveling back and forth in an endless stream. The Silk Road had reappeared, bringing prosperity with it. The historic traveler Marco Polo came to China in the latter part of the 13th century. He described in his travel notes the prosperity of the Hexi Corridor, as well as the influence of Buddhism there.

Left: Hevajra Buddha, Cave 465, northern wall

An Arhat, Cave 95, southern wall

The Yuan Dynasty came to be a great patron of Buddhism, attaching particular importance to Tibetan Buddhism. During that time, Vajrayana Buddhism (also known as Tantric Buddhism, or Mizong in Chinese) became the prevailing form of Buddhism in Dunhuang. The influence of Vajrayana Buddhism in Dunhuang is best represented by the statues and portraits from this school in the Mogao Grottos. For example, in the northern section of the Grottos is Cave 465, which has an atmosphere heavy with esoteric mysticism. This atmosphere is due largely to its murals, which were inspired by in style and content by the Tibetan culture. An altar is situated in the centre of the cave, and the walls are painted with mandalas, which are important symbols for Tantric Buddhism. On each slope of the ceiling are portraits of Buddha. The mural

Background Notes on Mandalas

A mandala is an image used in Vajrayana Buddhism. The word, which is from Sanskrit, refers to a circle, which symbolizes perfection or completeness. Inside the mandala is often a compete microcosm of the spiritual world. Though the name means circle, mandalas can be rectangular or circular in form. A deity or Bodhisattva is painted at the center of a mandala. Often mandalas have an inner area, painted with Bodhisattvas and Buddhist symbols. Around this inner area, there is an outer area where various Bodhisattvas or Dharma protectors are portrayed.

of Akshobhya, or the Immovable Buddha, on the eastern slope of the ceiling has the blue-skinned Akshobhya flanked by two minor Buddhas. These represent the Trikaya of Buddha, which in Tantric Buddhism is associated with the mind, body, and mouth. The Trikaya is surrounded by a number of Bodhisattvas. These images were all flatly painted in pure colors, such as red, blue, white, and green.

Only small numbers of caves were built during the Yuan Dynasty. Some old caves were also renovated, but not many. Most of the caves built during the Yuan Dynasty have ceilings like an inverted "U". In addition to having a niche excavated on the western wall, some caves also possess an altar in the center, like Cave 465. Others feature a ceiling shaped as an inverted "V" in the anteroom, and a flat ceiling in the main hall, such as Cave 462. Cave 95 has a central column with niches in and statues of the six-armed Avalokitesvara, attendant Bodhisattvas, and Heavenly Kings. These are the only remaining sculptures from the Yuan Dynasty. Very few murals exist from the Yuan Dynasty. However, they are exquisite, and are best represented by those in Cave 3.

Cave 3

Located near the middle of the Mogao Grottos, Cave 3 is relatively small, with a depth of a little over 2 meters. Its ceiling is in the shape of an inverted "U", and it has a niche at the back. An inscription on the lower portion of the northern side of the niche, says *"Ganzhou Shi Xiaoyu bi"*– "Painted by Shi Xiaoyu of Ganzhou".

While Avalokitesvara with a Thousand Hands and Eyes was important to Tantric Buddhism from the Tang Dynasty onwards, Cave 3 is the only one at the Mogao Grottos in which all of the murals are thematically linked to this Bodhisattva. In the center of the southern wall are there is a portrait of an eleven-faced Avalokitesvara with a Thousand Hands and Eyes, standing on the lotus pedestal. Such portraits of are not required actually to have thousand hands and eyes, as how Avalokitesvara is portrayed is left to the discretion of the artist. This portrait has 40 main hands, with other hands arranged in a circle behind Avalokitesvara like a splendid halo. To Avalokitesvara's west are a Brahman and Daughters of Brahma-Heaven, while on the eastern side are portraits of Sakra and daughters of Brahma-Heaven. In earlier murals, Brahmans were usually portrayed as ugly-looking, naked, old heretics. However, this Brahman looks distinguished and friendly.

Another eleven-faced Avalokitesvara with a Thousand Hands and Eyes was painted in the middle of the northern wall, beneath which are Ganessa (Vinayaka), wearing elephant-like and hog-like crowns. To Avalokitesvara's east are Vasudeva and Dharmapala Vajra ("The Vajra who protects the *dharma*"). To the west are Dharmapala Vajra and flying *apsaras*. Dharmapala Vajra has six arms, all holding various symbols of *dharma*, including a *vajra* bell, a *vajra* mallet, wheels, and swords. He bristles with anger and looks awfully frightening. The *apsaras*, on the other hand, bear lively, noble expressions as the fly through the air with flowers in their hands. All of them wear crowns with floral hairpins, and loose skirts with feather-like sleeves.

Next to the door on the eastern wall is Avalokitesvara distributing wealth to the people. From his hands flow gold coins and ivory, and a poor child is catching them. To the south of the door is Avalokitesvara tipping a flask of nectar so that the man below him can drink of it.

The highly skilled artistry for depicting figures in this cave deserves praise. An example of nearly every drawing technique from ancient times

Avalokitesvara with a Thousand Hands and Eyes, Cave 3, northern wall

was used in the murals, for excellent effect in highlighting the costumes and even distinguishing the different cloths, such as brocade, silk, cotton, and hemp. The artists also used line drawings for a naturally rich and graceful effect in depicting the appearance of the figures. Like frescoes, these murals were painted on wet walls with muted colors, further highlighting the impact of the line drawings.

The Decline of the Mogao Grottos

In 1368 A.D., Zhu Yuanzhang established the Ming Dynasty and constructed Jiayuguan Pass, just 35 kilometres inside the western border of Suzhou. The rule of the Ming Dynasty extended just as far as the Jiayuguan Pass, leaving the vast western area–and Dunhuang–unprotected, and allowing ethnic minorities to freely settle where they wished. Buddhism, which had prevailed in Dunhuang for over 1,000 years, vanished in this region, and the Mogao Grottos, once regarded as a holy land by Buddhists, was devastated. The prosperous Mogao Grottos of the past lingered on in a constantly deteriorating condition.

In the third year of the Yongzheng Era of the Qing Dynasty (1725), Dunhuang County was established and placed under Qing rule. Immigration from areas inside of Jiayuguan Pass resumed, the wastelands were once again put under the plow, and the economy of Dunhuang experienced a resurgence. Since a number of immigrants were Buddhist, the religion once again acquired vitality. At the time, Mogao Grottos were shabby and dilapidated. Therefore, during the Jiaqing Era of the Qing Dynasty (1796-1820), large-scale renovations were conducted, with more than 200 caves of the past dynasties undergoing renovations. A handful of caves, such as Caves 11 and 228 were newly constructed. However, the original art of the renovated caves was damaged by the inferior craftsmanship of the Qing Dynasty restorers, while the newly-built caves boasted little of artistic value.

It was not until 1900 that the Mogao Grottos, forgotten in the sand for hundreds of years, once more saw light. This came through Wang Yuanlu's accidental discovery of the Cache of Manuscripts in Cave 17. However, the corrupt Qing Government did not carry out any investigation of unearthed cultural relics at the Grottos for more than ten years after the Cache of Manuscripts was discovered. Even worse, no effective protection policies were adopted in Dunhuang, causing a great loss of precious cultural relics to foreign collectors, many of them sold by Wang Yuanlu himself. A great number of manuscripts and artifacts from Dunhuang were looted one after

Background Notes on Aurel Stein

Stein was a British archeologist of Hungarian extraction. Under the auspices of the British Government, he conducted three explorations in Central Asia. In 1907, Stein came to Dunhuang, and left with 24 crates of ancient manuscripts, and 5 crates of silk paintings, fabrics, and other artifacts found in the Cache of Manuscripts. He capitalized on the ignorance of Wang Yuanlu, the Daoist priest looking after the Mogao Grottos, to buy the materials at a very low price. On a second trip in 1914, he obtained about 570 more manuscripts from Wang. Most of Stein's collection of the relics and manuscripts unearthed in Dunhuang during his three explorations to Central Asia are preserved in the British Museum, the British Library in London, the Indian Library of General Affairs, and the Indian National Museum. His publications include, *Serindia: Detailed report of explorations in Central Asia and westernmost China* (1921), *Innermost Asia: Detailed report of explorations in Central Asia, Kan-su and Eastern Iran* (1928), and *On Ancient Central Asian Tracks: Brief Narrative of Three Expeditions in Innermost Asia and Northwestern China* (1933).

Outer wooden structure of Cave 431

another by Oldenburg, a Russian; Stein, a Hungarian-born Brit; Pelliot, a Frenchman; and a Japanese exploration team led by Otani. As a result, more than 10,000 manuscripts and pieces of art work from Dunhuang found their way to Britain, more than 8,000 to France, and over 10,000 to Russia. It was not until 1910 that the Qing Government ordered all of the remaining Dunhuang cultural relics to Beijing, to be held in the Beijing Library under the watchful eye of Chinese scholars.

Background Notes on Paul Pelliot

Pelliot was a French sinologist and archaeologist. From 1906 to 1908, he excavated several Buddhism sites in Bachu and Kuche of Xingjiang Province. When he came to the Dunhuang Mogao Grottos, he numbered most of the caves, copied down the inscriptions, cut a great number of murals from the walls, and smuggled out many relics unearthed in the Cache of Manuscripts. Pelliot's collection of Dunhuang manuscripts is preserved in the French National Library. His artifacts from Dunhuang are kept in Guimet Museum.

Cultural relics from Dunhuang were thus scattered overseas, catching the attention of scholars around the world. A new branch of research, Dunhuang Studies, emerged, and the remote area of Dunhuang became known worldwide. With this increased attention, the popularity of Dunhuang as a topic of research and study exploded. In 1944, the Kuomintang Government established the Dunhuang Research Institute. In 1950, the People's Republic of China made it a priority to augment research of the caves and to enhance their protection, rechristening the Dunhuang Research Institute as the Dunhuang Research Institute of Cultural Relics. During the 1960s, although China was suffering from an economic depression, the central government still allocated a huge amount of money for a large-scale project to maintain and stabilize the caves, saving many which were in severe danger of collapse or irreparable damage. Caves at the Mogao Grottos were linked with each other by plank paths, and walls, doors, and windows were added to the fronts of the caves to shelter the art within. Since the 1980s, the doors and windows have been improved further, and glass screens have been installed in many of the caves open to the public in order to protect them from visitors. The Mogao Grottos are now listed as a World Heritage site, further promoting the research and preservation work at Dunhuang.

However, the protection of the Dunhuang Mogao Grottos is still an arduous task. After having experienced more than 1000 years of difficulties

Background Notes on the Otani Exploration Team

This exploration team was initiated and organized by Japanese Buddhist abbot named Otani Kozui. From 1902 to 1914, the team visited most of Xingjiang and Gansu, investigating and excavating Buddhist relics. They collected and looted a large number of cultural relics from Dunhuang, Turpan and other areas. Many of these cultural relics are kept in the Kyoto Museum, at Ryukoku University and in other places in Japan. However, since they were not able to take all of their relics back to Japan, some are preserved in the Lushun Museum in China.

Remains of temples at Dunhuang Mogao Grottos

and hardships, both visitors and researchers are concerned about whether Dunhuang can possibly stay well-preserved for long. The staff at the Dunhuang Research Institute of Cultural Relics has devoted their time and energy to the study and protection of Dunhuang cultural relics. Their work has been supplemented with the help of UNESCO, allowing for the development of cooperative research regarding Dunhuang between China and other countries, such as the U.S.A., Japan, and Canada.

In terms of the future direction of preservation efforts at the caves, the director of Dunhuang Research Institute of Cultural Relics reports, "The effort to protect the Dunhuang Mogao Grottos has shifted from the early stage of rescuing, to that of scientific protection. Ultimately, it will evolve into a kind of precautionary protection, based on our massive achievements in the scientific study of preservation. Avoiding the destruction of cultural relics in the first place is the primary goal of the scientific study of the preservation of cultural relics."

Research in Dunhuang studies has made great achievements during the last twenty years of China's reform and opening up to the outside world. Prior to the 1990s, it was often said that even though Dunhuang was a part of China, China was not a leader in Dunhuang studies. This belief has become outdated in academic circles, as China's scientific research of Dunhuang is now the best in the world. On the other hand, some famous scholars, led by Ji Xianlin, hold that Dunhuang research belongs to the world. They wish to emphasize the international characteristics of Dunhuang research, opposing isolated research in Dunhuang studies, advocating international collaborations instead.

While the Dunhuang Mogao Grottos belong to China, they are also a cultural heritage of mankind. Its treasures are opened up to welcomed visitors from all over the world.

Xia Dynasty	c.2100BC- c.1600BC
Shang Dynasty	c.1600BC- c.1100BC
Zhou Dynasty	c.1100BC- c.221BC
Western Zhou Dynasty	c.1027BC- c.771BC
Eastern Zhou Dynasty	770BC- 256BC
Spring and Autumn Period	770BC- 476BC
Warring States Period	476BC- 256BC
Qin Dynasty	221BC- 206BC
Han Dynasty	206BC- 220AD
Western Han Dynasty	206BC- 25AD
Eastern Han Dynasty	25AD- 220AD
Three Kingdoms	220AD- 280AD
Wei	220AD- 265AD
Shu Han	221AD- 263AD
Wu	222AD- 280AD
Jin Dynasty	265AD- 420AD
Western Jin	265AD- 317AD
Eastern Jin	317AD- 420AD
Northern and Southern Dynasties	420AD- 589AD
Southern Dynasties (Song, Qi, Liang, Chen)	420AD- 589AD
Norther Dynasty	439AD- 581AD
Sui Dynasty	581AD- 618AD
Tang Dynasty	618AD- 907AD
Five Dynasties	907AD- 960AD
Song Dynasty	960AD- 1279AD
Northern Song	960AD- 1127AD
Southern Song	1127AD- 1279AD
Yuan Dynasty	1279AD- 1368AD
Ming Dynasty	1368AD- 1644AD
Qing Dynasty	1644AD- 1911AD